PENGUIN BOOKS
SURVIVING MEN

India's best-selling author Shobha (Rajadhyaksha) Dé was born in Maharashtra in 1948. In the course of a career in journalism, she founded and edited *Stardust*, *Society* and *Celebrity* magazines and is now a popular columnist and an author of nine books.

Shobha Dé is married and lives with her family in Mumbai.

Also by Shobha Dé:

Socialite Evenings
Starry Nights
Sisters
Strange Obsessions
Sultry Days
Snapshots
Second Thoughts
Uncertain Liaisons *(with Khushwant Singh)*

Shobha Dé

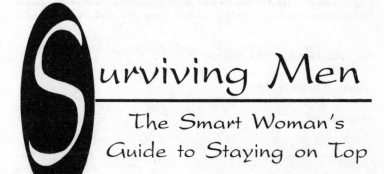

Surviving Men

The Smart Woman's Guide to Staying on Top

PENGUIN BOOKS

Penguin Books India (P) Ltd., 11 Community Centre, Panchsheel Park, New Delhi 110 017, India
Penguin Books Ltd., 80 Strand, London WC2R 0RL, UK
Penguin Group Inc., 375 Hudson Street, New York, NY 10014, USA
Penguin Books Australia Ltd., 250 Camberwell Road, Camberwell, Victoria 3124, Australia
Penguin Books Canada Ltd., 10 Alcorn Avenue, Suite 300, Toronto, Ontario M4V 3B2, Canada
Penguin Books (NZ) Ltd., Cnr Rosedale and Airborne Roads, Albany, Auckland, New Zealand
Penguin Books (South Africa) (Pty) Ltd., 24 Sturdee Avenue, Rosebank 2196, South Africa

First published by Penguin Books India 1997

Copyright © Shobha De', 1997.

10 9 8 7 6 5

Typeset in *New Brunswick* by Surya Computer Services, New Delhi

Made and Printed in India by Swapna Printing Works Pvt. Ltd.

Just Kidding . . . .
Love Ya Anyway

To Dilip . . . .
For Surviving Me

ontents

Introduction

Introduction

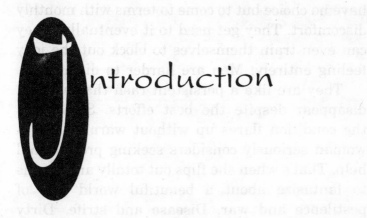

ntroduction

A normal, healthy woman has to live
with menstrual cramps for upto
thirty years of her life. If not longer.
That's four days each month for
three hundred and sixty months. That is some
thirty-four thousand, five hundred and sixty
hours of discomfort and dull pain. Compare that
to her life with a man. Same time-frame. Similar
pain. Which would she rather give up if she had
the choice—men or menstrual cramps? I guess
you know the answer.

Women are strange creatures. They feel
possessive about their PMS. They also feel
possessive about their men, but unlike cramps,
which eventually go away . . . men don't. Not as
easily or as predictably, at any rate. Women

have no choice but to come to terms with monthly discomfort. They get used to it eventually. They can even train themselves to block out the icky feeling entirely. Men are harder to dismiss.

They are like a persistent rash that will not disappear despite the best efforts. Sometimes the condition flares up without warning and a woman seriously considers seeking professional help. That's when she flips out totally and begins to fantasize about a beautiful world free of pestilence and war. Disease and strife. Dirty socks and hairy chests. Wet bathrooms and beer breaths. Lousy sex and joint accounts. And, chiefly, this man. Maddening.

Even the most inflamed case of hives can be treated—or tolerated—provided you know how. (A smart woman doesn't scratch. She doesn't bleed. And she doesn't cry. She stays on top. Of the rash, of everything else. And then she gets on with the rest of her life keeping her hands free for attending to something more useful than an itch that refuses to leave her.)

But what do you do with a man?

Only two women and one man have read the rough proofs of this book. Said Renuka, the film-maker, 'I wish men would come into our lives all potty-trained and house-broken. Why don't you add a chapter on getting them there?' Prita, my editor, looked up from the pages she had so meticulously marked and commented tersely, 'Dumping. You've left out dumping.' So

I had. The nameless man responded with his customary cool. 'Yeah,' he said, 'yeah. You have a point.' Well, thanks. I was kinda hoping I did. Several, in fact.

Those were the professional opinions.

Floodgates opened up when I casually mentioned the subject of the book to others. Strange women would sidle upto me and hiss, 'Show them. Finish them off. Fix them, the smug sons of bitches.' And I'd go, 'Huh?'

This book isn't about 'showing' them or 'fixing' them. Heck no. Men are okay. It's just that women are more okay. Men don't know that, of course. Which is also okay. We don't *want* them to—see? That would ruin everything. Women are subversive, sly beings who thrive on stealth and secrecy. They have a complex, varied rich inner life most men do not so much as suspect exists.

That is our strength. And revenge. So long as we can cling on to our fantasies (the favourite one involves murdering the spouse), life chugs along in a well-greased groove. It is when we surrender our dreams and get real that problems surface. Big problems. We start analysing our mates. Our 'situation'. Our futures. None of this adds up to a pretty picture. Anger and frustration happen. Fights happen. Issues happen. Divorce happens. Mucho mess happens. Women get stuck with the short end of the stick. And women don't like that. They pick up their end of the stick and try and beat the guys with it. Now, guys don't like it. Nobody likes being beaten. It ends up with everybody hating everybody else. Life becomes a bummer. Finally, men and women declare in unison, 'Marriage sucks.' The rash disappears. A new one appears—this one is called terminal loneliness. Nobody wants to be lonely. Nobody likes being lonely. Everybody decides to be 'sensible'. Sane. Slimey. Is it a cop-out? You bet it is. So, what are the options?

'Mine is a Post-It marriage,' a young woman in her late twenties tells me. 'My husband and I work our butts off. We hardly get to see each other. I often have to work through the night. He leaves those cute little yellow notes on the fridge for me—I do the same for him. That's how it works.'

Sure. For how long? I want to tell her, yellow notes, no matter how cute, are a poor substitute for a warm bed and an even warmer meal. But this is a modern, urban Indian marriage involving modern, urban Indians. They do their bonding over washing machines and personal computers. Hired, part-time help runs the house. Relationships are sealed or broken via e-mail and faxes. There is no downside—unless you count divorce.

Who packs the dabbas? 'Do it yourself,' growls the exhausted wife. 'Why can't you pack mine for me?' the husband whines. 'Because I don't ask you to pack mine,' the wife snaps. The man appeals meekly to the *bai*. She rolls out two chappatis, warms up left-over veggies and he's off. But at least his wife is rash-free for the day. And her *bai*-packed dabba is ready to go, too.

'I bring in as much money as he does. I work equally long hours. I hate it when he offers to "help" me fix dinner. What does he mean by "help"? It's such a presumptuous word. It indicates he has assumed making dinner is solely my responsibility . . : and he is being kind enough to share some of it with me. Bullshit. We both have to feed ourselves. As far as I'm concerned he does his bit and I do mine. It's a joint effort. No favours.'

No favours? This woman needs help. She needs this book.

Since *Surviving Men* reveals well-guarded male (and female) secrets, I'd say keep your mind open as you read on . . .

We love making a super production out of fairly simple things like, like—like a man who routinely beats us up. We like to *talk* about it, for heavens' sake. Not merely dismiss the whole business with a grunt and a 'Men!'.

If you can understand a woman's genetically programmed need to talk, and talk some more, in fact, never to stop talking—even if it means going without sleep, food and sex (in that order)—you'll figure out the *raison d'etre* of this book.

Men don't talk as much. Perhaps it's because they're too mean—even with words.

Are all men stingy? Ummm—I'd say generally so. That's because men secretly and not so secretly believe that all women are out to take them for a ride—even those who earn far more than they do. Chat up a guy in a bar (yes, honey, it's perfectly all right these days. Everybody is chatting up guys at bars—even other guys) and sooner or later he'll load you with his money problems. If he is married, he will wiggle his eyebrows as men do when discussing their wives (it is a gesture intended to convey that she's pretty but foolish. Or not so pretty but bossy) and say something like, 'I don't know about you but my wife can't resist a bargain—any bargain. Last week she bought forty kilos of detergent because it worked out cheaper in the long run. But what about the money I had to shell out up front for it?'

Yes, we know money is power. The person who controls the purse-strings plays grand puppeteer. If the wife is wealthier, she's the one who makes the husband beg for pocket-money. A painter friend chortles with glee as she recounts a neat reversal of roles in her marriage. 'For years it was my husband who made me crawl for a few thousand bucks. He'd ask for detailed accounts and make me justify each piddly purchase. Well, now that I'm a successful artist and he my manager, the ball game has changed. I can tell you I make him work really hard for his supper.'

Men and their money, are rarely parted. Watch them stuff wads of notes into their wallets. Watch the manic look in their eyes as they regard those crisp bank notes, saliva dribbling down their chins. You want to tap them on the back and say, 'Hey. Relax. It's only paper.' Not that they'll get it. Money acts like an aphrodisiac on men. That may explain why men are horniest at the beginning of the month when their pockets are full. The libido starts sliding seriously as expenses mount and the bank balance shrinks. Women understand that. They like money as much—especially their mate's.

Very few men encourage this trait. Those who do, end up broke. Not that women are incapable of handling funds—they do a great job in that area provided there are no questions asked. Unfortunately, men don't trust them sufficiently. There are two specific areas that men hate to leave to women—the care of money and the care of their genitals. Men tend to guard both zealously, going to the extent of throwing themselves belly down on a bed to pre-empt a frontal attack. Men with genital infections/injuries would rather risk castration than allow a woman to dress the wound. The ideal money-pouch, therefore, is the one slung in the male crotch, protected from the wandering fingers of avaricious predatory females. Men would invite death before parting with a farthing. And guess what—most women wouldn't care to stop them either—provided they can get their hot little hands on that farthing.

Men are also convinced women are disadvantaged when it comes to understanding basic economics. This applies to both married men and singles. A bachelor may appear to be humouring his girlfriend when he comments, 'Neelam is so . . . so . . .' (he yearns to say 'dumb' but doesn't). 'She just can't get the hang of the market.' At this point it's best to leave it at that and not get into 'Which market? The financial one or Crawford?' For if you do, you are likely to be stuck with a twenty-minute monologue on what happened when Neelam and he went shopping for a car/gas range/four-door refrigerator/after-shave/panties. You definitely don't want to get into this.

Men like the act of doling out money to women. It makes them feel magnanimous and charitable. It also makes them look like mean bastards—but they rarely stand in front of mirrors when they're handing over 'house money'. Women hate these moments—and men love them.

There is only one way to get even—rip the s.o.b. off. It's worth taking a few leaves out of Ivana Trump's book. When the chips are down, raise the stakes. If you play your cards smartly—bingo—you'll hit the jackpot. Miss the chance and you've blown it for life. Some women live by the motto: A man and his money must be parted.

It's not such a bad motto when you figure the odds.

Men go to extremes to conceal their true worth, their precious incomes. Any smart woman with a nifty Japanese calculator can figure it all out. But it's best to play dumb and act broke— even if it is hard to shame a man into reaching for his cheque-book—particularly if you've refused to put out.

Do women really want to take men for a ride? Listen—don't tell anyone I said this—the basic, honest answer is 'yes'. I can hear a collective male cry going up—'We knew it. Now it's official!' Why do we do it?

Well, I think it's one way of getting even. A poor substitute for the real thing (murder or castration) but it makes a woman feel so much better if she has managed to take some money off a man (why not? Since he has probably deprived her of her self-respect and maybe her virginity too?). Women who earn hundreds and thousands of rupees in perfectly respectable careers still get a kick out of stealing a few bucks from a guy. It gives them a sense of achievement quite out of proportion to the petty amount they've managed to extract out of their men. The triumph lies in the act itself—the fact that they've succeeded in parting Mister Scrooge from his carefully hoarded notes, generally stashed away in an old shoe (or some place equally obvious).

Most men break out into a virulent rash when women so much as mention money. They get a cornered, guarded expression in their eyes which indicates a panic-attack is imminent. The reaction goes right back to their childhood—or so psychologists tell us.

Moneyed men are no different. Their miserliness exceeds known parameters of acceptable conduct in public. It's worth watching them in action at, say, a Diwali card party. Loaded movie stars burst into tears, great big tears, on losing twenty bucks at rummy. Meanwhile their wives, shuffling away at adjoining tables, play on recklessly and win.

What happens when the couple gets home at five in the morning? The husband demands his share of the goodies. The wife generally tells him to bugger off—it was *her* win, remember? At which point he bars the bathroom door, refuses to let her pee and bellows, 'Bitch! It was my money you were playing with.' The wife coolly removes her jewels (bought with his money), undrapes her saree (ditto), removes her make-up (paid for out of stolen 'house money') and goes to sleep. Does the dumb cluck continue to stand by the bathroom door? Yes—for another hour or so. And then he cries some more.

Why are men such misers? Ask their moms. They'll tell you how their munnas used to hide filched marbles in biscuit tins when they were kids. Or recycle underpants as teenagers. Moms can be indulgent about their sons. But nobody (least of all a wife) is amused by a mean-minded guy.

But, as I said earlier, men are okay. Except that most women prefer pets—puppies or parrots. If you, however, have to live with a man, it's best to undertake the exercise with humour and pre-knowledge and God on your side. Remember, no optimistic man will ever consciously resist getting to know a woman. Any woman. Men are hopeful creatures.

They are also fairly easy to train. It's only a matter of mastering certain basic commands ('Down boy') and techniques ('Yes, it is a *terrible* headache'). Once you possess the key, the rest becomes a cakewalk . . . men being transparent, gullible, slow animals. The trick is to not let them know (*ever!*) that you know that. If you can do that convincingly enough, it's possible to live with them. Even love them (just a little).

If you're married and a woman, make sure your husband gets his hands on this book months after you're through with it and have mastered a few survival tricks. If you are male and single, memorize certain key chapters before getting into the next relationship. Married males are advised to seek expert medical opinion before going ahead—especially if they're forty plus— the book could give you a hernia and/or heart trouble (I guess most men would settle for the latter). And if you are a single lady—keep this by your bedside and use it as a guide to avoid falling into the man-trap (it exists).

Surviving Men is about staying on top. Staying ahead. And maybe winning the lifelong battle of the sexes. (The book is, after all, addressed to women.) As in everything else—it's the toughest who smile as the men in their lives trudge off to fulfil their time-ordained roles as providers. Just you relax and let the poor fool do his bit toiling in the fields or at a work station. Your job is to concentrate on bigger things—like the next down payment on that darling farmhouse in Mehrauli. Or the Concorde trip that never happened. Give him a loving squeeze now and then to let him know he's around and appreciated (he'll settle for even less—but why short-change the fellow?) . . . but don't, for heaven's sake, lose focus. Play the nurturer's role to perfection, keep your personal goals in sight and enjoy yourself. A crabby, ill-tempered, whacked-out woman ends up poor and alone. Well-timed smiles and a hot meal are impossible to replace. When all else fails, try instant gratification via sex, cuddles, massages, poems, shoulder rubs, cold beer, compliments and kebabs. Whatever works, as they say. That is . . . if men are high on your priority list.

If not, then read the book for reassurance. If you're single and deliriously happy, you'll know what you aren't missing. And you'll be able to hug yourself, smile a secret smile and exclaim,

'Saved!'.

I am a great respecter of deadlines. To me, they are sacred. But I nearly didn't make this one. The reason? Just as I'd concluded I'd covered it all—every wart, mole and beauty spot—I'd be up against fresh insights, additional inputs. Was this book never going to end? Would I be writing it forever? 'You're still on a learning curve, baby,' someone said helpfully. That's when I knew I had to stop or I'd be updating the manuscript for the rest of my life. They say one lives and learns.

It's a never-ending process, I agree.

Men live. Women learn.

The

Question Of

Man

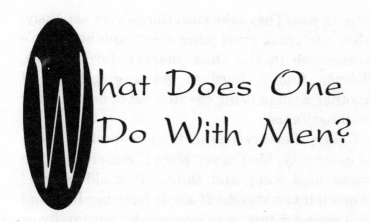

What Does One Do With Men?

Several things, actually. One feeds them well. Pampers them occasionally. And even tries to laugh at their jokes. Seriously.

Try this sometimes. Sneak up on a group of guys knocking back their vodka tonics at the club bar. Listen to their conversation. Try and understand their humour (such as it is). Find it funny? Nope. And yet the men obviously do.

So . . . is there something wrong about a woman's sense of fun? Umm, that depends on whose side you're on. Men generally laugh at other men. Their jibes are aimed at the imagined size of a rival's penis, for example. Women don't discuss the dimensions of other women's bra cups in jest. They take such things very seriously. Men also crack cruel jokes about another chap's misfortune in the stock market, for instance. Women find it hard to get a giggle out of another woman being cheated out of her alimony or inheritance.

The difference lies in their respective levels of insecurity. Men never place themselves in the shoes of a loser and think, 'It could be me.' Women invariably do. If a wife loses her husband to a younger tart, gets dumped by her family or misses out on a major career break, other women will sympathize, at least on the surface—not crack jokes.

Why? Because they're gentler and kinder? Certainly not. Fear. That's it. Fear that if it could happen to her, it could happen to any one of them. Maybe as soon as tomorrow. Men who laugh together generally drink together. Women who do the same generally share nervous tension. To get a good handle on male humour it is important to know what makes men laugh (besides the imagined size of etc. etc.). Basically it is relief. When a man can look at another man and say to himself. 'Thank God that isn't me,' you can be sure he'll split his guts laughing. Men are also vastly amused by slapstick situations. Someone slipping on a banana peel. Someone else running for a bus and missing it. A third, oversleeping and skipping an important appointment. Screw-ups are a turn-on for men.

They get their biggest kicks from watching a fellow man make an utter ass of himself, preferably in public.

Women rarely find humour in real-life situations. In fact, they rarely find humour. Which is why you don't get that many women doing comedy or even living it. Women's laughter is restricted to sharing anecdotes about their childrens' antics. Join a group of happy-looking women at a party and chances are they'll be discussing what their kids have been up to. Don't get me wrong. It's not as if women are totally devoid of a sense of humour. They do laugh—at men, for instance. But never in groups. And never at themselves. Laughter is a private act, a much needed release. Laughter is reserved for those precious moments when they're by themselves (something that only happens when women bathe). That's when they allow themselves a few malicious chuckles which, though they are far from funny-funny ha-ha, generally act as a much-needed safety-valve.

Giggling men look foolish. Women feel proprietorial about giggling. They hate it when grown men usurp their privilege, since they sincerely believe they have an absolute monopoly over giggling. That doesn't stop men from indulging themselves in a giggling session now and again. But, they should be told, it drives women crazy. Especially since giggles generally follow twenty rounds of beer. Which is why women naturally associate booze with giggling. And no matter what they say, women (wives in particular) hate the fact that there are several occasions when the men in their lives will willingly forsake them for a barrel of beer. Which is why, if you're a man and if family unity matters to you at all—don't giggle. If however, the urge to do so over-comes you, rush towards the nearest, softest cushion and smother the giggle before she smothers you—yes—with the same cushion.

Some men laugh for no reason at all. They laugh because laughter feels good. Or the TV programme is boring. Often, this catches a woman off-guard. And women as a rule resent being caught off-guard. They feel there is some sort of cheap trick involved and that makes them suspicious. Is the man who is cracking up in bed actually disguising a heart attack? Or does the laughter signal bad news of another kind? Maybe he's about to tell her he's leaving for the Maldives with her best friend. Or that he has just been fired. She doesn't know. But in any case, she doesn't like it that he should be laughing so hard at nothing in particular. She also imagines (often rightly) that he's laughing at her. This may send her rushing to the mirror—is her lipstick smudged? Has she forgotten to wear it? Are her eyes crossed? Has something large and furry suddenly sprouted out of her head? For men who find it necessary to giggle/

belly-laugh/roar, a word of friendly advice—warn her in advance, or better still—leave the room first.

Other than laughing at them and occasionally with them, there are several things one can actually do with them without inviting murder. One can (i) watch Prannoy Roy on *STAR News* (ii) copulate while watching Prannoy Roy on *STAR News* (iii) bathe together under a waterfall and copulate while Prannoy Roy continues to read on *STAR News* (iv) read in bed companionably while watching Prannoy Roy on *STAR News* (v) sleep together as distinct from engage in copulation.

Men can be useful in trying social situations. They are good when it comes to clobbering pedestrians who dart across the streets on moonless nights; not bad at fixing drunken louts on the make; excellent at dealing with bellboys, courier peons and airline clerks. They do have their uses after all.

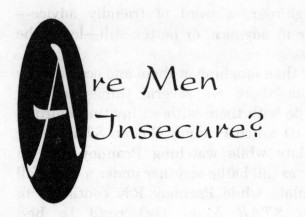

Are Men Insecure?

Of course men are insecure. And who wouldn't be? They spend almost their entire lives fighting insecurity. Some do it more convincingly than others.

Try and catch them unawares at, say, an airport. Observe them as they walk past glass showcases. Seven out of ten will check if they still have the same amount of hair on their heads as they left their homes with. Keep watching. As soon as the flight is announced, the men displaying high hair anxiety will whip out tiny pocket-combs and run them rapidly through whatever it is that's on their heads. Balding men seem even more fanatical about fixing their sparse strands. Notice also the extent these chaps often go to in order to camouflage their 'condition'. I'm not talking about toupees, hair weaves or corn-row transplants. I'm referring to the seriously hair-disadvantaged. Some of them grow extra long strands to arrange neatly over the shiny spots, others wear caps indoors, while a few decide to brazen it out by going all the way—that is, by shaving it all off. There is yet another category—the ones who grow beards as a compensation.

Maybe hair fixation has a lot to do with men's concerns about virility. Maybe they really believe the Samson story. Maybe they think all women are closet Delilahs. Rubbish. As it has often been pointed out, some of the world's sexiest men have been bald. Or short, or both. What has been left out in this charming observation is a vital piece of information. Those guys have also been loaded. Gold-digging ladies don't have the slightest hesitation when it comes to choosing between no-hair-and-lots-of-money and lots-of hair-and-no-money. In other words, hair has nothing to do with it. Sex appeal lies in the wallet of the beholder. Like I overheard a Sindhi gentleman commenting about his future son-in-law, 'My wife advised my daughter to pay more attention to the guy's balance-sheet than his biceps.' Sorry girls, but the truth (such as it exists) must be told. Women are self-seeking and greedy. And perfectly capable of looking beyond the bald pate at the beach condo in Goa.

However, since it's men we are worried about, let it be known that the bald ones have problems which have nothing to do with women. Why else would they stick enormous cigars into their puckered mouths? Examine the pictures of cigar-chomping celebrities in magazines—nine out of ten Havana smokers in the world are bald, or getting there rapidly. If these fellows were even remotely concerned about the effect of foul cigar smoke on most women, they'd know that it is a major turn-off. They aren't smoking to impress women. They're smoking those ugly things to distract everybody's attention from their bald heads.

Chest hair or the absence of it, doesn't seem to obsess men in quite the same way. It might interest them to know that women on the other hand have strong views on this. Girls like hairy guys. But not furry ones. There is a distinction between hirsute and shaggy. How much chest hair is too much hair?

Since at this point it's important to instruct by way of living examples, why not use Anil Kapoor as a prototype? That man ought to be banned by law from baring his body. His torso resembles a tropical forest or an unmown lawn. Hair of such density is definitely not sexy.

Women don't like a marble-smooth finish either. Body hair should be evenly distributed. It helps if the growth isn't concentrated in either the ears or the nostrils. Hairy legs à la Andre

Agassi (before he turned into an aero-dynamic tennis machine) are interesting. Hairy backs aren't. Men seem to have cottoned on to some of this, going by the numbers at beauty salons across the world where they are unabashedly getting the extra fuzz tweezed, waxed, bleached or threaded. They're also having some of it dyed . . . which isn't such a smart thing to do when you look at some of the awful colour jobs floating around. Haggard, jowly men with jet-black, blow-dried, stiffly sprayed heads of hair are almost as grotesque as haggard, jowly women with jet-black, blow-dried etc. But who can convince the hopefuls?

Men should worry less about their hair and more about their gut. It's true. Women will settle for wispy-haired specimens provided their bellies are as flat and taut as hardboard. Paunches, as it might be pointed out, tend to get in the way. Beer bellies cannot be condoned or ignored. Flab isn't funny. (But nor is an Adonis with muscle where some grey matter should've been.) Spindly legs? Will do, if the intellect glows. Pigeon chests? No problem, if the conversation dazzles. Non-existent butts—there'll be some takers at a pinch, if the eyes are seductive enough. But a gut like a bloated blimp? No, no, no. In other words, boys, start touching your toesies right after you've mastered toddling. There is no substitute for heavy-duty exercise, alas. And how long can any man humanly hold his breath and tuck the tum-tum in without bursting?

Men should also pay more attention to their teeth and oral hygiene. It's an area that most 'how to' books tend to ignore. Well . . . don't. The mouth is after all, the gateway to a myriad pleasures starting with . . . smoking (just kidding). Stained teeth and puffy gums tell you quite a few things about a man. The chief being his aversion to flossing. Couples who floss together stay together. Flossing can be the day's most intimate activity not counting . . . errr . . . breakfast in bed. Gleaming teeth declare their owner's fastidious attention to detail. A man who spends sufficient time on his cavities is the, sort of man who'll hold your hand during a root canal procedure or a molar extraction. He's been there. He knows.

We need good teeth. Our digestion depends on it. So does fresh-smelling breath. Men with bad breath (we'll come to b.o. later) cannot possibly be good lovers. And if they fail in that department, they fail as husbands too. So . . . it's simple. The secret of a successful relationship lives in the drilling abilities of a good dentist. Great teeth equal great sex. Give or take a few incisors.

It's time to move down a bit. And get to basics. Men worry about their genitals excessively, women don't. About men's genitals, that is. Actually, they don't worry too much about their own either. Only when they have a post-partum tear or an infection. As Freud told us a long time ago, little boys get fixated on their pee-pees from the time they leave their mama's warm wombs. Ask any male kid, he'll tell you he prefers his own teeny-weeny G.I. Joe to the moulded plastic fella. It is definitely not so with little girls, mainly because they can't play doll-doll with their concealed equipment. Besides, Barbies are more fun, with long blond hair to make braids out of and pretty party frocks to change. Little boys aren't so easily pleased or distracted—not when they have an in-built toy to play with. Something soft, squeezable, non-complaining and, chiefly, unbreakable (unless subjected to violent abuse such as attempting to sharpen its point with a knife).

Penis-fixation is pretty hard to shrug off and don't believe a word of what new age psychologists tell you. Observe men at work or even men not at work. Chances are at least one of their two hands will be in the general vicinity of the crotch. (And it's only poor Michael Jackson who gets all the flak.) Scratching is a form of meditation. It helps them to focus. Concentrate. But mainly it makes them feel good. It also reassures them that their G.I. Joe is still around and functioning. If you believe it's important to recognize and accept your mate's little idiosyncrasies, treat his, ummm, thingie with respect. Do not, repeat, do not, manhandle it, even. in a fit of passion. You may get away calling his mother names, doing a Sharon Stone on his boss, buying an outrageously priced gew-gaw for the house or even borrowing his shaving cream. But heaven help you if you make fun of his private parts.

Men can (and often do) spend hours relating to their 'friend'. It can be a purely unconscious activity (like while watching a cricket match), or one designed to give instant pleasure (first thing on waking). A wise woman ignores such infantile behaviour and concentrates her energy on something more worthwhile (like extracting additional 'house money' while the good mood lasts). Or flying the idea of a Bali vacation for the entire family over X'mas. If the request is timed right, i.e., when the man has a glazed expression in his eyes as his fingers keep busy, chances of victory are pretty high. The woman who understands a man's need to communicate with that part of his anatomy is a clever woman, even though she, on her part, does not experience the same need to, say, tweak her nipples now and again to see whether they're still there.

So what? That shouldn't make her feel superior or anything. It's differences like this that make the man-woman business such a business—for all those over-paid Agony Uncles and Aunts for example.

What else does it take to send a man

scurrying for his security blanket? I'd say career worries, though they feature far lower in the anxiety-ladder than his genital-fetish or hair-mania. Men worry about their careers like women worry about their—no, not housekeeping money—but future security. The two are interlinked. The more a man worries, the more insecure his wife becomes. A vicious circle is formed in which the man strives to hang in there and provide for his family and the woman wakes up at night wondering whether there'll be a roof over her head six months down the line. Both fears are grossly exaggerated. There is nothing half a tumbler of a peaty single malt can't resolve (provided the man doesn't have to hawk his life insurance policy for a bottle).

The best way for a couple to tackle anxiety is to go on a holiday together (the bills come later). In salubrious surroundings (Seychelles is high on the list for couples with money problems), everything melts away (including what's left in the bank account). Only a foolish woman will choose such magic moments to bring up silly, inconsequential topics such as . . . say, the son's college fees or the next down payment on the car. No, an attitude like that ruins everything—mainly the man. We don't want that happening to us.

Good timing is an integral part of good strategy. Open your mouth at the wrong moment and phut—you blow everything. Let honeyed words drip over a chilled Chablis as the moon rises over the Andes (oh, all right—the Western Ghats) and the man surrenders. That's the official script.

Of course there are spoilsports galore who refuse to play ball. Well girls, these guys don't deserve you in the first place—right? Nothing works with men like these. In a similar situation, it's wise for a woman to start thinking seriously about another option—a new roof. Or a new man. There's no point losing valuable sleep-hours wondering about one's roof—especially if you live in a city that experiences a heavy monsoon. It's also important to recognize a simple truth—men *like* to worry about money. The more they have of it, the more they worry. They will tell you with a logic that is so male it has whiskers, that it is precisely because they worry about money that they have it.

This is probably true. But women are bound to ask, a little stupidly perhaps—if men are constantly worrying about money how can they possibly enjoy it? Men have an answer for that as well. Money, they'll assure you, is not for enjoyment. It is for investment—and that's precisely why women are *so* lousy at handling resources. They believe, idiotic as it is, that the moment women get money in their hands, they feel obliged to spend it. The faster the better. It's as if they think a wad of notes is really an explosive device with a timer attached to it.

Keep it in those eager little hands for even a second longer than absolutely necessary and chances are it will blow you apart.

Men, on the other hand, go to extremes to hoard money. It hurts them physically to spend it unless they're going all out to impress someone—a woman, in most cases. Most men develop a dull ache in the region closest to the heart when they're confronted with bills—their own included. This is because they have a collective memory that takes them back to pre-historic times. The moment they have to reach for their credit cards is the very moment they remember the hostile environment beyond the security of their caves, when they were forced to roam the wilds in search of berries and suchlike for the greedy woman back home.

Smart women are pretty good at getting men to reach for their wallets. The trick is to make a man believe you are way beyond his financial reach. The moment a man thinks he cannot afford you, he'll willingly flog the shirt off his back (along with more valuable assets like . . . like blue-chip shares that go for the price of a suburban flat in Mumbai or a Bikash canvas) to prove a point to you. The thought that there could be another chap with deeper pockets is really what motivates men to make utter fools of themselves.

Let them. It's part of their being men. It makes them feel great. Who are we to deny them such harmless pleasures, especially when we are the beneficiaries? Women who extract huge fortunes out of men adopt another even slyer trick—they behave like they're doing the men a huge favour by accepting their money. This way, they get both, the lolly as well as the man's eternal gratitude. By being kind to a man with money to lavish on her, a woman displays not just uncommon shrewdness but far-sightedness as well. The kinder she is, the more generous he gets. Generally speaking.

But don't count on it. A mean s.o.b. reveals himself early on in the relationship. The sort of guy who buys you zircons and calls them diamonds. Or mixes local whisky into bottles of Scotch. Or leaves measly tips for waiters he knows he's never going to see again. Or argues with taxi-drivers in foreign lands about fares and currencies he knows nothing about. Or insists on buying half-a-dozen polyester ties in place of two great silk ones. Or stinges on laundry bills in hotels, preferring to wear horribly creased shirts. Or brags about conning an innocent and/or ignorant widow out of her property/Ming vase/priceless jewellery/family heirlooms. Such men can never turn into honourable chaps no matter how good the woman is to them. Rather, the odds are they'll take shameless advantage of her kindness (feigned or genuine) and make her beg for scraps.

Men do get instant amnesia when it comes to

remembering favours—big favours. A woman may spend twenty years of her life slaving for the guy, washing his undies, keeping track of his stock of shaving cream, cooking exotic meals, making sure the kids stay out of his hair, massaging his head/feet/something softer on demand, putting up with sudden and entirely unannounced noxious gas explosions in the bedroom, tolerating the sight of him concentratedly picking his nose/teeth/belly-button while reading the newspapers, leaving heaps of wet clothes all over the bathroom floor, kicking off his shoes any which where and expecting her to pick up after him, firing servants for minor misdemeanours, and not noticing that it has created an extra load for her, interrupting her phone conversations with sisters/friends/parents without the slightest embarrassment, and the worst offence of all—demanding (and getting) sex on call. The most wild-mannered men turn into foul-mouthed louts when turned down in bed.

Men like the status quo. It suits them. Why should they be in a hurry to change anything when every conceivable facility is being laid on for them? This is where women frequently err. They believe (rather tragically) that men notice such things. And more—that men actually appreciate them. Not true. Or if some men *do* notice they make pretty damn sure not to let their partners know. Why? Ask a man and he'll promptly tell you—'Give women a little power and they'll misuse it.'

Power? Misuse? What are they talking about? They'll tell you what, in lucid terms. Women have to be kept in place at all times. Show them appreciation and they'll use that as leverage. Ignore them and their output will double.

This is probably true. Women are simple in some respects. Pay a woman a compliment and she'll immediately ask for something—often something ridiculously small, like tickets to the cinema. Or a bottle of perfume. Or a pressure cooker. More fools us. For what follows next isn't fun. The man starts feeling like a potentate and behaving even worse. He makes the woman feel about as high as Thumbelina after magnanimously sanctioning her tiny purchase. The debt cycle begins all over again.

People say the New Man is different. He recognizes his partner as an equal and gives her the respect she commands. Ask around. Ask a few couples—you know the couples one means— not those miserable creatures in some suburban colony whose idea of a great time is an outing to a neighbourhood chaat-shop on a scooty. Choose your couples with care. Look out for all the giveaway signs. The status symbols. The clichès. Start with the clothes. Does the man believe in Friday dressing? Does he combine safari khaki wth cerulean blue? Does he roll up his shirtsleeves even when he's got on a tie? Does he favour shoes with laces to slip-on loafers? Is his bathroom well-stocked with beauty products for men? Is it after-shave gels he goes for over regular lotions? Does he know his Thai from his Vietnamese cuisine? And, pay attention to this, does he approve of the idea that shaved armpits are a distinct lifestyle option for women these days? Yes, to everything? All right then, maybe he has earned his Dolce and Gabbana G-strings.

But watch out for this fellow all the same. He could turn out to be a very tricky customer. And no different from the chap who at least didn't pretend to be better. The New Man has only learnt new tricks, that's about all. He is essentially the same old s.o.b. recycled in a sharp suit. And if he's a smooth enough operator, he can fool even the New Woman (who may be less wide-eyed than her elder sisters, but still a novice when it comes to men). The New Man's brand of manners works on a different level. He fights over C.D.s and L.D.s, not pressure cookers and rice-makers. He insists on his woman paying for her half of the holiday, right down to splitting the tab on a round of Tequila Sunrises. He believes in his and her haircuts even when they go to a unisex salon together. This is his way of defining equality and he makes no apologies for it. But then he doesn't have the slightest moral compunctions when it comes to her paying for the cellular phone service that he uses or for club facilities that suit him more than they suit her. He just ignores these little inconsistencies and accuses her of being a small-minded bitch if she dares to bring them up.

In this respect the 'traditional model' is vastly preferable. What you see is what you get. And often that is depressing enough. But at least there are no catches involved. You don't like his attitude? Well, baby, take it or leave it. Which is fair. The other stuff is more insidious. You don't like his attitude? Well, baby, guess what? It's yours that's out of sync with today.

Generous men do exist. (But, they tell us, so did dinosaurs.) Several of my girlfriends will vouch for it. Chances are these guys are generous only because they suffer from awfully low self-esteem. They sincerely believe they have to present platinum credit cards to the woman they wish to bed. But generous men make women suspicious. The first question they ask themselves is: what's wrong with him? Is he normal? Does he have a shrunken . . . ummm . . . ding-dong? Bad breath? B.O.? Hernia? A mother? All of these? It is somehow not natural for a man to loosen the purse-strings without expecting something in return. This 'something' is not always sex-related though chances of it being so are pretty high. It could be just the opportunity to be seen in public places with a flashy/well-known lady.

Whatever. The catch remains. Mating games or matrimony, it doesn't change the rules. A generous husband is generally a stupid husband who can't express his gratitude differently. It's his lack of imagination that makes him cover his beloved with diamonds and pearls. A smart man sticks to compliments . . . and sex. Most women are idiotic enough to settle for flattery in place of a flat.

This isn't good thinking. Ideally, she should aim for both and get them. Real life works differently. A husband with honey on his tongue and money in his own bank account is no better than a confidence trickster, but try telling that to the woman he lavishes exaggerated praise on and she'll call you jealous. Women are silly that way.

Jealous? Of a hairy, old toad who calls his wife sickening things like 'poodley-doo'? There are men who adopt more subtle tactics, of course. Recite poetry or, worse, write some themselves. Send no-occasion flowers, celebrate birthdays, remember menstrual cycles, count the moles in their girlfriend's armpit, fetch iced water on cue and tell her the moon gets a complex when she's around. Most probably she'll fall for the bilge and forget the nasty business of the time he told her firmly but oh-so-sweetly to pay her share of the phone-bills. Or shell out money for the new TV set which he would control by locking up the remote panel before leaving for work.

Even the toughest woman turns into a marshmallow the moment a man tells her how beautiful she looks in blue or something equally inane. I know a canny business lady who chews nails for breakfast, but turns into a cocker spaniel pup in the presence of fawning male admirers. 'I could drown in those eyes of yours,' gushes an insincere lout and she promptly lets him. The compliment stays with her long enough to distract her from the deal she is about to clinch with a buyer from Lagos. Fortunately, her native money-sense asserts itself eventually and all goes well.

There is a lesson in there for all of us: choose your compliment-giver with care. And settle for the one who is willing to open a joint account.

How Men Deal With . . .

listen guys, this chapter may embarrass you. If you'd like to skip it—go ahead. Actually, it's rather a humiliating one. I mean—you think you've been dealing with this book manfully so far, right? Well, guess what? You haven't. You know why? Because you've been reading it and saying to yourself, 'Oh man. This is crazy stuff. It's stupid. And, in any case, it isn't about me at all. It's to do with all those other moronic men out there. Yeah—like that asshole boss of mine. My brother too. And all those club fellows hanging around the bar. The losers. Me? In this book? Give me a break. I'm not in it. I'm different—you know? Like, superior. I don't fall into the stereotype. I don't indulge in all the crappy stuff this woman is going on about. Know what? I think she's crazy. Out of it. That's right. She has seriously lost it. I mean, what a load of bull this is.'

It's okay for you to slam the book shut right now. It's also okay for you to skip the next few pages and find the good stuff. Yeah, the good stuff. It's there, somewhere. Only, you'll have to look hard, real hard, for it.

Fine.

How do men deal with . . .

Anxiety: Pretty much the same way they deal with practically everything else. They pretend it doesn't exist. They play ostrich. They hope it will go away if they ignore it. What do guys get anxious about anyway? Ummm, mainly hair loss (I swear that's what a survey recently revealed) and money-gains (never high enough). The more they worry about their hair, the more of it they lose. Sometimes they worry about other stuff like serious debts, death in the family, cardiac arrest, losing at golf. But mainly it's about hair doing the disappearing act. They have ways to duck issues that make them distinctly uncomfortable. Who likes to think about constipation, for instance? Nobody, right? But only a fool won't pop a few extra prunes into the system if it becomes a chronic thing . . . and the prunes ensure instant relief. They (don't ask 'who'?) say women are generally more anxious than men. Naturally, they have men to be anxious about. Read *Cosmo* if you don't believe me. According to Helen Gurley Brown, women have just one thing on their minds—men.

How to trap them, keep them, leave them. And all this stuff makes women awfully anxious. Life is easier for men—why should they worry about getting a woman out of their hair when there *is* no hair to get her out of? Men also get anxious about their beer bellies—when that happens, they walk to the nearest ice-box and help themselves to another bottle, beer being definitely high on the therapy-scale.

So what *do* men really, really worry about? Chiefly about their private parts. If there's any time left over, then they worry about the future. But even here, their private parts manage to creep in ('Will I still be able to get it up when I'm fifty-five?') A man who is physically attacked invariably covers his crotch first and then protects his head and heart. He can't help being anxious about his genitals. His sense of self dangles between his legs.

Tension: Men insist they never experience it. Mention the word and they holler, 'Tension? What's that? What tension? I'm not tense. Woman—don't do this to me. *I am not tense!*' If you observe men when they reach this point, you will notice veins that rival pipes throbbing menacingly on their foreheads. Their eyes will bulge. Their hair (what's left of it) will stand up. Their neck muscles will be strained. Call that tension? Nah. They don't. They're just being men. And yes, expressing themselves somewhat strongly.

Catch them at a cricket match (a live telecast will do). Same symptoms. That's not tension, they'll remind you. That's excitement. Adrenalin surging. The usual man-stuff. *Right*.

Climbing up the corporate ladder may give the impression of tension happening but they'll emphatically state it isn't so. Tension, even hypertension, involves serious denial. The more men pretend they don't suffer from it, the more their bleeding ulcers misbehave. 'It's not tension that's causing those buggers to corrode my intestines—it's the bloody chillies you use in the food,' they'll bark. In other words—*You are the cause*. Try talking about A-type personalities. Men will glare . . . go eyeball-to-eyeball. And then leave the room. Which is why a woman should never raise the subject of tension on an airplane. Men are known to ask for parachutes just to escape the T-word.

Sorrow: There is nothing in the world that cannot be solved by something that makes the sound of glug-glug-glug. Booze is the ultimate equalizer. Men turn to the bottle when all else fails. Alcohol is the answer to all problems— even existential ones (Sartre? Sartre?). And since the poor guys are denied the release public tears sometimes bring, they are compelled to seek other ways of dealing with tragedy. Some eat. Some drink. Some sleep. But mostly, they drink. A man with a secret sorrow seems to turn on countless women (Guru Dutt in *Sahib Bibi aur Ghulam*). A sad man without a drink in his hand looks incomplete. As if an essential prop was missing.

If you notice one whose hands look kind of at a loose end, do the chap a favour—buy him a drink. Buy him several drinks. But don't marry him. Sleep with the tragedy king if you want to (though sorrow-plus-alcohol adds up to lousy sex) and then get on with the rest of your life. Sorrow draped like a dark cloak around a gloomy figure crouched over a highball in a dingy bar is admittedly seductive. Sorrow is capable of converting a boring fool into a brooding sexy Nicholas Cage . . . even so, it's best to leave the brooder to his booze. People who weep and tank up together, rarely stay together.

Woman handle grief more sensibly. They beat their breasts, they wail, they cry, they starve, they pray, they punish themselves . . . till one fine day they discover the grief has vanished. Just like that. It's out of their system. They are whole. Ready to face the world once more. Expressing deep sorrow isn't macho, according to men. You lose a wife, you lose a child, and you lose a parent. You lose a friend, you lose a colleague, you lose a pet—but you don't lose yourself. Never. You keep calm as you walk around your mother's pyre (ref: Rajiv Gandhi at Indira's funeral) and swallow the tears manfully. Shoulders straight. Eyes dry. Voice steady. If you are breaking into a thousand pieces inside, that's really too bad—but the world doesn't particularly want to know about it, okay? However, just as real men are once again being seen in public eating quiche, they are also allowing their tear ducts to function normally. Which is just as well. If there's one thing worse than a sad man who cries, it's a sad man who doesn't.

Stress: Men love it. They thrive on it. They all but live off the stuff. If there was any way for some canny entrepreneur to bottle and market stress successfully, he'd stand to make millions. Men believe stress is good for them. Which is why they like to refer to women as 'complacent cows'. They're so happy they're not either, see? Not complacent. And not cows. They're happy being stressed-out maniacs with glazed expressions and electrocuted smiles. Stress and success go hand-in-hand—in men's dictionaries. The higher they go, the worse their stress levels get. Do they care? Not at all. Stress is meant to be worn like a badge—proudly. Stress indicates the state of their business (and busy-ness). No stress? No sweat? Man—are you a loser or are you a loser?

There can be no real happiness in life without

stress. Nobody wants to look like the meditating Buddha—blissed out. Walk into any health club and watch those animals as they punch bags, lift weights and stretch muscles. Check the eyes. Crazed. Check that muscle mass. Scarey. Pumping iron isn't about body-building. It's about laying stress on the line.

The chicks love it too. Who needs a control freak when you can have a Brad Pitt clone? Way to go, desperado. But of course you can enrol for a six-week Reiki session. Meditate in the mountains. Get your own mantra. Focus on a mandala. Go in search of a guru. All that is an essential part of the attractive stress-package. To feel good you have to feel like a dog. Even look like one. Stress is great for your sex-life too—and forget what the experts say. Just ask Mick Jagger groupies—they'll tell you.

Surprises: Don't spring them on someone you love. Men loathe being taken off-guard. There is nothing that drives them as berserk as an unexpected call/gift/message/visit. Remember, we are dealing with programmed limited creatures incapable of improvising or innovating. More often than not, what you see is generally what you get. No tricks. We, with our devious minds and crooked ways, take time to understand this. We adore the unexpected—especially when the unexpected comes from the mines of de Beers.

Men react to surprises like they're been given a particularly nasty shock—like 400 bolts from a substation. They go to the extent of sniffing gifts. What to they think the package contains— explosives? And even if it does—are they trained sniffer dogs?

Women dislike including men in gift-choosing sessions. Women believe they know what's best for their man. Big mistake. Men treat gifts like transactions—you like, you pay, you buy. They don't think it is unromantic to fix a prior appointment with their loved one, march her off to an impersonal store, ask her to pick something in a specified range—and then pull out a card to settle the amount. Ugh. The other choice is leaving it to them. Still more ugh. Imagine a puke-green saree with purple peacocks dancing on the pallav—why even Govinda would refuse to be seen in such a combination (or would he?). Men have strange notions about colours—seen some of the latest ties? You don't need shades to look at them, you need a blindfold.

Since surprises are a no-no, and men shudder at the very word, how does one celebrate a special occasion with a guy? Take my word for it, hon—leave it to him. The tabs included.

Do Men Have Feelings?

J t is assumed that they do. But nobody has been able to actually prove it so far. I believe men have feelings the same way dogs have feelings. I came to this rather startling conclusion after certain basic observations: eye movements, the twitching of nostrils when an alien object (woman) is seen approaching, heavy breathing while engaged in anything strenuous (sex, for example), a whining sound when the belly aches (usually after over-eating)—and, of course, the loud barking at all other times.

Going by irrefutable evidence like this, it can be safely deduced that men do experience something closely resembling feelings as we recognize them to be. But don't ever make the mistake of expecting normal reactions to standard stimuli. Men are completely incapable of responding to the distress of small children, for example. They do a good job of pretending, however, especially if they have tough wives who expect them to behave like the New Age men so frequently featured in magazines. That's when they have clearly no choice left but to rush to an infant (generally their own) that's about to choke to death on a large bead fed him by another infant (not necessarily their own, but frequently so). Left to themselves, men would look up absently from their files/papers/magazines/books and go back immediately to the paragraph that required re-reading. But with society's pressure weighing heavily on them these days, they have to first adjust their expression to register alarm and concern that they don't necessarily feel and then actually rush to pick up the thing in the pram that's rapidly turning blue, and try and remove the obstruction from its throat. All this is done without much feeling. In fact, if men were to be honest (it's awfully hard for them to be, but a few do make a sincere effort), they'd tell you that the feeling uppermost in their minds at a time like that is fear—fear of their wives.

Once every two or three years, men realize they haven't felt a thing for a long time and make a conscious decision to do something about it. They ask their secretaries to jot the point down. Or they write a short memo to themselves. Peep into a male's filo and chances are you'll spot it on top of the agenda. 'Feel something,' it will state. And the man who has written it will try very hard to do just that for at least a couple of hours. The effort will prove to be too much and he'll give up, satisfied that he has given it a shot.

Don't blame your guy too much if he doesn't feel. Primitive man didn't feel either. He hunted and he procreated in a mechanical way. Things haven't changed all that much since then. Men go off to their offices, come home, have sex and go to sleep. Millions and millions of men, on a daily basis. They don't complain. They don't crib. They aren't missing anything. They accept life as it is—programmed and predictable. It's women who spoil everything by bringing feelings into the picture. The two words (in any language) that spell disaster are 'Something wrong?' Men ask it conversationally. They don't really want to know. Women misunderstand the question. They start from the top of their list of grievances and five years later, they still haven't finished. Some women can keep at it for thirty years and more. If you interrupt them and ask 'Why are you going on about it?' they'll look at you like you're stupid. Because the man asked, they'll say. If he didn't want to know, they'll fume, why the hell did he open his mouth?

They have a point. Women shouldn't be asked such an obvious question. They probably already have the answer and don't particularly like it.

Men, on the other hand, are incapable of responding to words of concern. Try it for yourself. Ask a man, 'Something wrong?' right after his house has burnt down, he has been fired from his job and his wife has left him. He'll look up pleasantly, shake his head, shrug and say, 'No, nothing's wrong. Why do you ask?' He isn't snubbing you. He isn't telling you to mind your own business. He is genuinely puzzled by the question since he has never asked it of himself. Besides, he cannot imagine another person being even remotely interested in matters that concern him alone. He's also not accustomed to sharing problems with anybody. When people discuss male bonding, what they're referring to is men boozing. Since men don't believe in secrets, there's nothing to pass on. They also think they can handle whatever it is entirely unaided and on their own. So, asking them a question like, 'What's wrong?' is a stupid mistake. Nothing is ever wrong with men. They're always 'just fine', 'couldn't be better' or 'great'.

Does death affect them? Yes. For approximately ten seconds. And that too if it's likely to cause an immediate problem in their schedules. Say, someone in the family die suddenly. A man's first thought will be, 'Oh hell—I'd better get the travel desk to reschedule my flights.' The token expression of grief will follow only after all the other appointments have been reslotted. Does this make them heartless? No, it makes them practical. 'Everybody has to go at some point,' a man will say cheerfully at his mother's funeral. Women will be weeping into their hankies remembering the time when they were small and mother had always been around to hold and comfort a frightened child coming out of a nightmare. Confront a man with this scenario and he'll be indignant. 'I loved my mother, damn it,' he'll splutter. 'I don't have to make a public exhibition of it.' Well, someone might point out, going to a cocktail party the same night and joking about the event is likely to mislead people. The man will now look hurt. 'That's my way of dealing with the loss. Besides, I know that's what she'd have liked me to do.'

Sure.

Besides, grief is a girlie emotion. Real men don't cry over coffins. They cry into drinks. Real men maintain a stiff upper lip when their sweetheart's run over by a car. But they weep gallons over a dent in the fender. Or when they're asked to pay a fine. Or when their favourite trousers get inadvertently burnt by a careless iron. Or the worst calamity of all—their underwear gets chewed up by the dog. Men cry big fat tears over tax returns too. All other teary occasions are reserved for breast-beating women and kids in wet diapers.

Men have feelings. Just like earthworms have feelings. Scientists who monitor such stuff have confirmed that when electrodes are placed on the skin (of men and earthworms) and a mild current is passed, twitching takes place—proving without the slightest doubt that there *are* feelings in there. But you don't have to take any switch-happy scientist's word for it. Try the experiment for yourself—but make sure you don't accidentally electrocute the fellow. One can't be too careful with electricity.

Women sometimes wonder, what touches men? Ask around and you'll discover it's the simple things of life—a handsome set of golf clubs, a well-crafted pipe, André Agassi winning Wimbledon (or not winning it, depending on how highly the man thinks of Agassi), a sexy sports car, a mellow whisky, well-made curry, an expensive fountain pen, a state-of-the-art computer . . . things. Men tend to get really, really attached to their possessions. Far more than women do. Burrow into old trunks and battered suitcases—you'll find all sorts of strange mementoes going back forty years. These could include frayed jock-straps and mouldy vests. Try throwing them away. The man will lie on his back and yowl. He'll also physically restrain you from doing any such thing. Don't fight him. He'll wrestle you to the ground if he has to. The best strategy is to gently replace the lid and walk away from the rotting muck inside. And, oh, yes—don't make the mistake of referring to it as 'muck' either. Unless you want the man at your throat ready to throttle you for insulting his past.

Does this prove that men are sentimental at least about their jock-straps? Not really. Men hang on to their 'things' because they are reminders of their lost youth and glory days. When they lovingly hold the stiff-with-dirt-and-age singlet in their hands, they are thinking of the runs they made wearing it, or the goal they shot. And they're feeling heroic. Their 'things' reassure them in a manner that you can't because you weren't there in the locker room when they climbed out of grubby clothes and showered with the team. And even if you were the sort who sneaked into the men's room to hug your guy, you wouldn't understand the deep meaning of that moment.

It's best to leave men alone when they regress and turn boastful. If you think it's going to be an extra-long session of reminiscing, open two cans of chilled beer and nod your head from time to time. He'll think you are listening . . . participating . . . cheering. And he'll forget to yell at you for not having that leaky faucet fixed or for misplacing his prized silk tie.

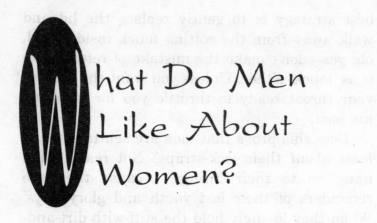

What Do Men Like About Women?

et's see. Most men would grin at such a question, get a lechy look in their eyes and declare, 'Everything.' Liars. Fact of the matter is, they like the *idea* of women—as an abstract concept, not to be confused with the real thing.

Women on the other hand make no bones about the fact that there's very little they actually like about men. But since their tolerance levels are so much higher, they find it easier to put up with the strain of living with them.

Men don't think about women all that much, unless there is a specific urge—generally sexual in its origin. Not that it is immediately recognized as such. Men do think about sex a lot (far more than women), but it's only when this thought gets focused that a face and body get attached to it.

Men will say lightly that they like the way women smell and feel. That's partly true. Men with sensitive noses will happily identify different smells and go into raptures talking about them. This is why the best-paid 'noses' (people who create top-selling perfumes by mixing different fragrances) are men. The perfume industry thrives because of men's obsession for the way women smell. Women use perfume to entice men. The promise is simple enough and rooted in the animal kingdom. Facetious types might deny this and cite Al Pacino's tango in *The Scent of a Woman*. Ignore them because they're only trying to side-track the issue. The smell men go for doesn't come out of a bottle at all. Women exude it naturally. It is sweet in a clinging, cloying way. And it's slightly sour too. That might explain the worldwide craze for Chinese sweet-and-sour dishes. They smell of women.

Experts say there are different scents men associate with the different body parts of a woman. Some men respond to flowery shampoos and reserve the stipulated one-and-a-half minutes of foreplay for burying their noses in their lover's locks. Others like the combination of perspiration, talc and cologne that lingers in the hollow of the woman's neck, while still other prefer to start at the feet and make their way up slowly—very slowly—resting midway through in the general region of the belly. This is where 'the scent' meets 'the feel' in a perfect marriage. Whatever Madonna might say about pumping iron and doing weights, all men (given the choice) prefer soft bellies to flatboards. Taut midriffs look great in publicity stills or packaged between the covers of a nudie-book titled *Sex*. But bellies like that don't work for real guys. Sorry, Madonna. But remember, girls, a little 'meat' is all they're asking for, not kilos of loose, flabby tissue.

Men also insist they like women for their 'softness' and 'sensitivity'. The truth is slightly different. Women aren't all that soft and sensitive—but why not let the poor buggers believe it? The perfect woman has to smell nice, feel good and be willing to match her man drink for drink. It doesn't always work as Meena Kumari found out in *Sahib Bibi aur Ghulam*. But it's worth giving it a shot. In addition, if the woman also cooks and cleans up afterwards, she's worth taking home as a permanent live-in domestic.

What do men like about women? Crudos will respond by coming to the point instantly: 'Isn't it obvious? They like a good lay.' That brings up another difficult question—what is a good lay? Rather, who is a good lay. Progressive, upfront women's magazines have attempted to answer that for decades. But nobody is any the wiser for it. Ask a man to elaborate and he'll shrug and say, 'Oh—I don't know. A good lay is a good lay.' Period.

Women will never tell you even if they've been told they are good lays by men—the best. Women are insecure about stuff like that. They actually believe that if they share their secret, the other woman will promptly practise it on her man and steal him away. They're probably right.

Nobody has been able to unravel the mystery of what exactly it is that makes a woman 'good in bed'. Archaeologists spent centuries deciphering hieroglyphs on pyramid walls in the hope that someone as accomplished as Cleopatra would reveal to the waiting world what Anthony discovered in her bed. But the wily old queen took the secret with her. And it couldn't just have been the asses' milk that did the trick.

Nobody knows what makes a woman etc. etc. Not even Helen Gurley Brown who threw the question at an unsuspecting readership years ago by asking it boldly on the cover of *Cosmopolitan*. She didn't provide any answers. So generations of women were left to agonize over the issue without anybody to illuminate them.

In their more candid moments (like, say, after six shots of tequila) women tend to confide.

But even in that mellow state, ask them what they do in bed to qualify and they'll instantly clam up. They don't want to tell you. Since men aren't much of a help either, I guess it will remain one of life's unsolved mysteries. However, for the sake of an interesting discourse, let's assume a women who is good-nay-great in bed is the one who makes a man feel like a champ when he's . . . er . . . doing it. How she achieves that is exactly what makes him a champ. Most women have their own little tricks which they'll refuse to part with even under threat of getting their titties tweaked. Don't waste your time asking them. You'll do better with men—even if they are so damned inarticulate and frustrating to talk to.

Actually, don't waste your time with them either. Women who've tried to pry this pricey secret out of even the most experienced studs have had to content themselves with a vague smile, a moony look in the eyes and a meaningful shrug. But an honest-to-goodness description? Forget it. Details aren't a strong point in this department. The day someone—preferably a man with countless conquests to his credit (Omar Sharif?)—decides to tell all, he'll become a billionaire.

And ruin it for the rest of us.

It's the guessing game that's exciting. Could it be the orgasmic shrieks in C-grade Hollywood films that drive men wild? Does that specific *sound* turn men on? Or is it love-words? Women on top? Pelvic thrusts? Low, appreciative moans? Back massage? Bites and scratches? Ear nibbles? Tongue? Eyes open? Eyes closed? A special b.j. technique? I suspect it's none of the above. The biggest turn-on in the world for a man is a woman's availability. Or at least, the promise of it. The thought that with a little persuasion a woman will jump into bed is really what makes her irresistible. That is the only possible explanation. Or qualification. Otherwise, given the limited (relatively speaking) options of what a man can do to a woman or she to him, the whole business of sex is entirely overrated. And the arbitrary scoreboard drawn up by experienced men, totally irrelevant.

Men assume women feign a lack of interest as a ploy—when really they're dying, just dying to 'do it'. Balls. *Some* women like to 'do it'. Some don't. Do guys recognize the diff? Hardly ever.

If women have mastered the art of masturbation, what stops men from following suit? Sheer laziness. They are far too spoilt to bother about jerking off. Why should they take the trouble, when they have obliging mates to do even that for them? Most wives complain that their men don't make love. Well—not to them. They only use their bodies to deposit sperm in. Having reached that goal, they go off to pee . . . often, just to ensure that little Johnny can piddle *and* procreate too.

Most men fantasize about the perfect b.j. Most women agonize over the same thing. To swallow or not? (*How Deep is Your Love* is more than just a popular song.) Kneeling down? On the bed? Five minutes longer . . .? Which way to the loo?

A woman who can successfully conceal her distaste for b.j.s and keep those lips moving is a woman who knows her true position in life; on her knees with her mouth doing all the hard work.

Men enjoy talking and thinking about sex far more than women. Women have better things to occupy their minds—like 'What's for dinner?' (even when they've cooked it themselves), or 'What do I wear to so-and-so's dinner?' (because of course, a woman never has anything to wear) or, 'Should I buy the blue sandals which go with nothing? Or the black ones which go with everything?' (the blue of course), or 'Is it time to bleach my upper lip yet?' (honey, do it daily, if you're serious), or, 'Will Babloo be able to get into college with his low percentage or will he have to join pappaji's spare parts business after all?' or, 'Why does that bitch have thinner thighs than I do even though she eats three aloo parathas for lunch every day?' (Darling, she sticks two fingers down her throat and pukes it all down the pipe, that's why.) This is major stuff. Sex? Hey—that's something you do on the side . . . not spend valuable time thinking about.

Women who take sex seriously are generally professionals for whom sex provides a livelihood. They'd better be good at it, or else it's bad for business. Men who like to pay for sex expect a certain minimum level of enjoyment that makes them feel good about the money spent. Nobody likes to invest in a dud product. But, like men will point out (fairly accurately at that), marriage too is a long-term investment in sex. What if the wife doesn't deliver? What if she refuses to supply on demand? Does he shrug it off as a miscalculation? A scrip that failed to live up to its prospectus? Cut his losses . . . and move on? Sometimes. But more often than not, men wisely decide that the best sex in the world is the one that occurs in their over-fertile minds and not in bed. It also happens to be the safest. Why take chances, they console themselves as they grab their erections and stroke away. Quite right, sigh their women gratefully. More time to watch TV and catch up on some sleep.

How To Hook A Man

Hey—every woman knows the answer to this one . . . and it does not lie at the core of a rotten, half-eaten apple, or wherever else they tell you to look for worm bait. Men are a lot like fish—dangle a line, and you've got 'em. In fact, most men resemble eager, greedy goldfish, bobbing around foolishly to keep those ants' eggs in focus. Notice carefully the next time. Watch the expression—those round eyes, that mouth, all puckered up and moving rhythmically. Substitute those ants' eggs. Try breadcrumbs. Same reaction. Men will go for anything— anything at all—if they think of it as a 'good deal'.

A smart girl learns to do her sums quickly. It

doesn't take much to figure out what exactly a man means by a 'good deal'. Most times it's code for 'good sex', even if he doesn't know that himself. A lot of women aren't ready to hook him this way (sex as bait comes later to her), so what does she do? Anything that grabs his admiring attention, but trick number one is to not let him know there is a hook. Hooks make men suspicious and wary. Worse, never let on that the hook comes with a load of paraphernalia. Your family, dog, ex-boyfriends, peculiarities. Catch him off-guard—and then vanish altogether. This is known as the old disappearing act. It always works. Men being slightly thick in these areas, they rarely recognize it for the ruse it is. The total duration of your disappearance has to be carefully timed and even more carefully monitored. No contact. No calls. When you know (how do you know? A woman always knows) he's in 'that' state—distracted, dazed, dopey—surprise him. Call him at work. Send a card. Offer to buy him a drink. He may just fall dead. Wait for a few seconds to find out whether he's still breathing. Repeat the offer. He'll bite. He has to. The fool is hooked.

A friend of mine (a fairly new acquaintance) relies completely on the femme fatale route. Here's her modus operandi: no man can resist a seduction, she insists. Given her amazing package, she speaks from a position of strength. Being a single bright female with impressive degrees in obscure subjects, she goes for the man's brains before attacking his you-know-whats. 'Once you've effed with his mind, he's yours,' she gloats. I dunno. I suspect she's been reading far too many American books of the 'How to Lay a Man-Trap' variety. Besides, there's not much a woman can do with just a brain if it isn't attached to something more valuable. Does Miss Femme Fatale go easy on the eyelash-fluttering? Heck no—she believes in the 'whatever it takes' approach. Most women do.

One of her less sophisticated counterparts put it more bluntly when asked what it takes to get a guy. *'Khaana, peena aur dena,'* she replied promptly. That is the way it has always been, so why should anything have changed now? Feed the guy's stomach, feed his ego too. Quench his thirst . . . (mineral water won't do it . . . poetry might. Good poetry).

And lay on the sex and food. Unbeatable. Look at the number of bestsellers cashing in on the combo. Films too. Remember *Like Water for Chocolate?* Men rarely close their mouths—so long as something is going in, they're happy.

Ditto for eyes. Women dress the way they do because they know about visual hunger too. Men are born voyeurs which is why lingerie ads turn them on far more than they do women. Left to themselves, women might go bra-less and panty-less. Or not pay such close attention to details (lace, ribbons, satin bows, underwiring) if it weren't for those popping eyeballs. Sexy underwear for women has been specifically designed to tease men. Girls who wear burgundy-coloured little things or wispy white nothings are the ones who know the game. The only 'secret' there is to pricey undies involves man's laser-gazed preference for a woman in her underthings to one in the altogether. Besides, it's a great feeling to wear aubergine silk foundation garments under a white shirt anyway.

Young girls don't have to worry too much about strategy. Youth is a good enough hook on its own. Great skin helps. So does a good bod. But there is no substitute for firm female flesh under twenty. Men know that. Traditional parents know that even better. Which is why teenage girls in rural India are forced to plait oil-soaked hair to remove any traces of wind-blown attractiveness, and forced into shapeless, unstructured garments specifically designed to flatten curves. No bounce, no trouble. The hooking game works differently in this context, with a premium on 'purity' (read: virginity). 'My daughter is very pure,' certify mothers to prospective in-laws, keeping one eye on the brand new Cielo parked outside. Nobody needs to decode that. It's understood. The 'boy' stares bashfully at his toes and instantly visualizes deflowering his pure bride on the wedding night. If the other factors weigh in (a flat, a micro-wave, a washing machine, shares and bonds), chastity wins the day. The deal is clinched over greasy laddoos. And one more *hymen intacta* gets sold to the highest bidder.

Phew! Isn't there an easier route? Don't bother with scintillating conversation—unless it makes the man scintillate. He really isn't all that interested in the Laxman Shrestha exhibit. Nor does he want to know whether *you* know who Shilpa Shetty is currently having it off with. Try telling him how wonderful he is and he'll be all ears (and all yours). Lie through your teeth about everything—including his receding hairline ('It makes you look so . . . so . . . intellectual. No, distinguished. That't the word. Distinguished'). A man loves nothing more than a worshipful woman at his feet—preferably one with boobs big enough to hide his boots in. Years ago I saw a beautiful, talented, exquisitely groomed actress sitting near the dirty chappals of an absolute lout—a paunchy, gross producer. The only time she moved away was to fetch him a refill. She made it to his bed—and the next blockbuster. Ten years later, I saw a repeat performance—she was older, the producer, much younger. Nope, she didn't get the role this time.

Wanton behaviour has its virtues and its followers. Some men get off on brazenness. They love women who talk dirty, come on strong and stay up all night on a rickety machan waiting for the shikar to begin. But these guys are in a minority. Most chaps are taken in by the coy *ghungatwalli* act. Know why? They delude themselves that they are the only ones who've ever lifted the veil and mesmerized the woman into submission. Conquest requires conflict. An easy lay is just that—easy. Men are constantly hungry—ravenously so. If they can get a quick nibble somewhere, they'll go for it. But even they don't confuse a spicy kebab with the main course—marinated *raan*. Women often confuse a quickie with commitment. That's not how it works. Hooking a man is easy enough, *keeping* him hooked, a lifelong game. Most women opt out once they've got their stereos, surround sound, silks, solitaires and stock options. If the guy wants to stray at this point, why bother? Let him. A preoccupied partner is better than an interfering one. If he's getting his regular nookie on the side, the housewife is rather relieved. It means she has more time and money for herself.

Marriage counsellors often stress the role played by the marital bed. It is this one single piece of furniture that determines the quality of the relationship, they say. Believe that at your own peril. Women who have used the beddie-bed as a hook have often been left there—alone and in tears. Men flee, never to return, if they smell the scent of another man in the bedclothes. Which is why courtesans remain courtesans—it is the coquettes who win big by teasing but not delivering.

Highly intelligent women often blow it in the hooking game by revealing their IQs. It is a known fact that most men prefer their partners dumb, stacked and great-in-the-kitchen (since feeding and uh-uhing go together). Brains are the scariest part of a woman's anatomy—the minute a man gets a glimpse of a brainy babe's grey cells, he goes into instant depression. It's almost as bad as actual castration. His self-esteem dives as he hides under the covers and tries to convince himself she's probably a lousy lay . . . so what if she knows her Pinter. Of course he can't get her out of his mind even if he does hate her. This is really the trickiest stage in cases where the brainy babe is serious. There are two ways she can play it—she could act dumb (and lose her USP) or she could be herself and take her chances. The second option is recommended (he's going to find out anyway if the relationship lasts).

Playing dumb has its merits provided you can keep up the act forever without cracking up. Frankly, no man is worth the strain involved. Brain power on motor drive can be both dangerous and potent. A liability and an aphrodisiac. Even brainy men (*particularly* brainy men) discover the hard way that they absolutely love brainy women—provided they belong to someone else. In other words—female brains are fun at cocktail parties, but no good when it comes to hook-and-keep.

Don't let that discourage you too much. Brains may not keep you warm on cold winter nights but at least they'll protect you from slobbering idiots drooling all over your cleavage.

Ever wondered why hookers remain hookers even though their main line of business is seduction? Because of that nasty word 'hook'. Women who are serious about getting their guy never let him suspect that what they're setting out to do is merely legitimize a modification of that old game. There are no rules here. Not really. Anything goes—even theft. Leave it to a woman to figure out the best method, be it sex, music, perfume, kinky games, Sardarji jokes, disco fever, Bacardi-on-the-rocks, mountain climbing, baby pink cashmere, bleached pubic hair, walks in the rain, the best biryani in the world. Demeaning? Naturally. But women, even illiterate ones, know that they outnumber men in the genetic pool. (There is only one way to fight this natural disadvantage—and that is by confusing the natural enemy into believing he's an ally.) The numbers don't always add up. But then who was it who said life is a bitch— without realizing how literal and loaded that little sentence is?

Women with the highest success rate in the hooking department are those who are talented and shrewd enough to make a man believe he is the centre of their existence. If they can also convince him that they are indispensable to his life—great. These are the ones who stay on top. Cleopatras without the asp. Apsaras worthy of being immortalized in frescoes. Learn from them all ye who wish to live forever in domestic heaven.

And learn from them, also, what *not* to do in order not to turn that heaven into hell.

There are five questions you should *never* ask men:

- Am I looking fat?
- How was dinner?
- What's wrong with my mother, anyway?
- Must you have another drink?
- What do you mean 'Where has all the money I gave you gone'?

Of course, there are five things you *should* tell men:

- Your hair looks just fine to me.
- That's not a paunch—your jeans have shrunk.
- No, I don't need any money.
- What about another one for the road?
- I'm ready whenever you are.

How To Dump A Man

on't think. Don't wait. 'Just do it'. Nike couldn't possibly be wrong. There is no nice way to dump a man. There is just one way—heave-ho and off you go. The sooner the better. Prolong the ordeal and remorse sets in. Guilt happens. You start feeling sorry for the sod. Marching orders must be given as soon as the drums begin to roll. Delay the dumping decision and write off the next decade: ten years of putting up with a turd you don't need. My advice: dump and be damned. But dump anyway. Make it swift, smooth, incisive—like precision surgery at its neatest. No scars either. At least, not on your person.

Don't even think about compromising. When your head (more than that silly little heart) tells you to move on—just get on with it without wasting a single second. The longer you delay the moment of truth, the worse it's likely to get. Men are thick and sentimental. They don't get the message swiftly enough. Often, they don't get it at all—even twenty years down the line. You have to be specific. And you have to be fast. Once you've blown the moment, you are a goner. It could take you two extra months or even two additional years to wriggle out.

Yes, they really are that dense when it comes to dumping. Which is why smart women tune in to the signals early enough and act with lightning speed when they have to. No lingering goodbyes. No tears. No explanations. No apologies. No post-mortems. Just a neat, surgical incision and *phatak*—it's over. The deed is done. The man is history.

Unfortunately, far too many women lack the all-important killer instinct. They put up with bullies, drunks, perverts, creeps and fellows with bad breath—sometimes for life—only because they don't know when to say 'Go'. Once that moment is lost, chances are the bum will stay. And you will teach yourself to lie back and enjoy him.

It doesn't have to be this way. Men who are bad news should be treated like putrefying garbage and discarded in the nearest bin. There isn't a reason on earth for any self-respecting woman to accept a swine or a slob—not even if he's picking up all the bills. Remember, he wouldn't be doing so if there wasn't something in it for him—sex-on-demand, food-on-demand, maalish-on-demand, clean underwear-on-demand, whatever-on-demand. Try withdrawing those essential services and then see the difference. Will he still love you tomorrow? Highly unlikely.

Men are creatures of comfort and habit. If they're programmed to expect khichdi on Monday, fresh pajamas on Tuesday, beer on Wednesday, keema on Thursday, tennis on Friday, golf on Saturday, more golf on Sunday and sex everyday—you bet they'll ask for it come hell or high water. Docile, obedient doormats are naturally reluctant to take chances just in case the guy ups and leaves. Well—that's fine if that's what works for you. It is when a woman does not want to perpetuate a rotten system, when a woman actively wants out, that the dilemma begins. How does she do it? How can she tell him? When should she tell him? Will he pay the slightest heed to her words? What tone is the right one? Straight talk or subtlety? Soft or hard? With sex or without sex? Over drinks, or over pakoras? In front of the kids or behind locked doors? Questions.

For young unmarrieds, it's relatively simple

and oughtn't to take more than a few seconds. It should be short and far-from-sweet. No more than two effective words firmly spoken—'Get out' (if you are a lady) or 'Fuck off' (which is the preferred dismissal). If the guy is too thick to get it and tries to cuddle you while you are pointing towards the door, a swift kick up his backside won't hurt. If he is foolish enough to attempt the old 'Aw . . . come on, baby, you don't mean that' routine, a slap or two may be thrown in for good measure. Since timing is crucial, make sure you are in your territory, not his, when you utter those irretrievable words. It's kinda *stoopid* to tell a man to take his sweet ass out of his own home. Make sure you are perfectly sober and haven't so much as sniffed at a glass of wine. Pop a stress-pill if you have to steady your nerves. Don't bother about how you look but it helps if you look irresistible. Say the words in front of a mirror a few times till you get your expression and emphasis just so. And then . . . and then . . . unleash them with all the passion you can possibly muster. Women who have delivered their lines successfully insist there is no greater pleasure in life. Not even the big 'O'. In fact, a blissfully satiated friend sighed, 'The only time in our relationship that the earth moved for me was when I spat out those two dreaded words that had been stuck in my throat for months.'

The softer option is to do it in a mawkish

sentimental fashion—with long, teary explanations, notes, flowers, candlelight and nostalgia. Forget it. Not worth the effort. The small, ugly business of returning letters, gifts, clothes, or retrieving favourite bras, shirts, jeans, sarees, perfumes and toothbrush from his place can be accomplished later, once the break-up has been formalized. Never confuse the two. First, announce. Then, retrieve.

The lingering break-up spread over years is even worse. Look, if you want to dump a guy, do it without making a bloody production of the break-up. Women who attempt to break loose in stages often end up saying, 'What the hell—how do I know it won't get worse with someone else?' This is a cheap cop-out. Besides being far more expensive and painful. I've known couples who've been breaking up for years only to find out that it takes far too much effort, so why not just hang in there and be miserable forever? You want that? You've got it. But if your priorities are to cut clean away and make your way in life without the burden of a bad relationship, waste no time, get on with the task. Treat it like a military operation—swift, efficient and victorious.

Women who weep all over their chiffons on account of the bastard they're stuck with, don't deserve the slightest sympathy—they deserve the bastard. If he's so awful why are they with him thirty years down the line? Ask them and they'll say piously. 'Because of the children.'

Lies. It's not the children at all. It's the money.
The solitaires. The penthouse. The granite loo.
The designer clothes. The status. The position.
The cars. The perks. A power-couple I know has
been talking divorce for twenty-five of their
thirty years of marriage. They squabble in public,
bitch constantly, come to blows in private, abuse
one another openly—but stay married. Ask them
why and they'll smile, 'Taxes.' Okay. At least
they're clear about their reasons.

Not so clear (or perhaps, not so cynical) are
the young marrieds—those who are already
disillusioned at thirty. Double-income, no-
children types. They agonize over the decision
in their smart barsaatis. And it's always the
woman who insists she's losing out. 'I want to
get rid of this pest,' she'll moan, 'but how?' The
pest is in no hurry to get rid of her. Why should
he be? She cooks for him, drives him to work,
cleans the barsaati, entertains wonderfully and
. . . you know the rest.

Dump him if you have to. But do follow some
basic dumping etiquette.

• It's bad manners to deliver a 'Dear John'
letter via e. mail or fax. Stick to a face-to-face
even if his face does make you go instantly
ballistic.

• Do not involve mutual friends in your
break-up. There's nothing worse than a taking-
sides routine where old friendships get carved
up and bartered.

• Don't go whining to his mother/wife/ex-girlfriend/best buddy/boss. It never works.

• Don't even think of hate-mail, blackmail or any other kind of mail, including letter bombs. Missives have a nasty way of backfiring on the sender.

• Don't trash his place in his absence or presence. He may summon the cops—or turn out to be a plainclothesman himself.

• Don't cut up his favourite clothes—leave that sort of stuff to Pamella Bordes.

• Use a reliable courier service to return personal belongings. Forget about despatching your baby brother to do the dirty work—he may not make it back alive.

• Voodoo doesn't really help. So throw that wax doll away.

• If you are the 'our song', 'our film' 'our restaurant', 'our hotel' type, go in for a refresher course—ideally with a refreshing new partner.

• Cold turkey is the only option known to work. Pick a Dumping Day. Maybe it coincides with your garbage-removal schedule. Get rid of both—the accumulated rubbish and the human junk, in one go.

Remember to celebrate.

You did it first.

Reason enough.

So fine. You've dumped the guy. You're feeling right on the top of everything. Powerful, strong. Free. Mainly, free. That's the happy part of the story.

But what happens when the driver of the dump truck is the chap himself? How does it feel to *you* to be discarded like a dirty dish towel that has outlived its use? Lousy—right? Lousy and wretched. Most women who check into the largest suite in 'Heartbreak Hotel' consider two immediate options: (a) Suicide (b) Another man. Both are equally self-destructive—the first one being literally so. By all means take your own life it that's what works for you—but not on account of a man. That's called throwing it away for free. No man, repeat, *no man* is worth the oxygen you won't be breathing after that last gasp.

And as for jumping feet first into another relationship, that's like chasing a streetcar named Disaster.

So how does a sensitive, caring, all-adoring woman get over the jerk who has waltzed away with her best friend/sister/mother? I'd suggest a long thoughtful shampoo—that's great strategy. Remember the old song from *South Pacific?* Rogers and Hammerstein said it all as Mitzi Gaynor trilled, 'I'm gonna wash that man right outta my hair.' Once you've had yourself a good cry, give the tear ducts a short break before turning on the taps again. During this brief dry spell, duck into a shower cabin and pour half-a-bottle of your all-time favourite shampoo over your head. Work up a lather (believe me, it beats foaming at the mouth) and let the suds do the rest. If your favourite shampoo smells of freshly-mown grass or a field of spring flowers, so much the better. Spend a longish time in the loo and ignore the brat knocking persistently on the bathroom door. You've earned your moment of privacy—don't let anybody, not even a pesky kid, cheat you out of it. It's amazing what a leisurely shampoo can do to a girl's spirits. Squeaky, clean hair has that effect on a low morale. Which is why women who are experiencing a bad hair day generally postpone taking any significant decisions till they've brushed out the kinks. You can't think straight when there are obstinate strands to deal with. Once your tresses are blow-dried and bouncy, your tattered love life will follow suit (yes, one can actually blow-dry tears too—try it). That's the time to take stock of the situation and arrive at a few sensible decisions.

Such as:

- Don't let your self-worth get any lower.
- Don't run yourself down.
- Don't keep saying. 'It's all my fault.'
- Don't stalk the lad.
- Don't make blank calls.
- Don't write pukey 'take-me-back' notes or poems.
- Don't beg for forgiveness.
- Don't re-read old letters.
- Don't torment yourself with icky memories.

• Don't put the rest of your life on hold, hoping he'll call.

• Don't demean yourself by asking for explanations.

• Don't attempt to 'make friends' with his new find.

• Don't stuff your face in frustration—you'll only gain weight, not sympathy from the other woman.

• Don't ask him, 'Where did I go wrong?' Ask yourself that instead.

• Don't visit old haunts obsessively, in the hope of running into him there.

• Don't jump into bed with his best friend/ brother/father. The deed is done. He is out of your life. You hurt. You hate. You suffer. Finally, you forgive. Which is all right. Women are generous. And foolish. Besides, they actually believe it's always their fault.

There is nothing like a dignified exit once the guy has stated he wants out. The more you cling, the more you mope. The more you weep, the further he runs. No babe, it doesn't work. Nothing really does. Pity is particularly unsexy— you don't need it. Self-inflicted wounds are for religious freaks and other maniacs who glory in scars. But you? Hey . . . you're ballsy and brave.

Of course, you've given the dog ten years of your life. Naturally, he is going to keep the fax machine, cell-phone, gold cuff-links, the bonsai collection, the L.D.s and the C.D.s . . . even your mother's gold chain. Let him. You hang on to your self-respect and share certificates (don't tell me, I know, it's a very poor consolation) and start working towards an oomphy tomorrow. Singledom has its upside. Think about it. You could still be with that roach. What?? You like roaches? Well then. You deserve to be dumped. Even roaches have their standards. They stay miles away from stuff that isn't good for them. And remember—these are the critters that will eventually inherit the earth. Nothing, not even nuclear fallout can erase them. They are the indestructible ones. It's a shame one can't say the same about poor, miserable, shameless you.

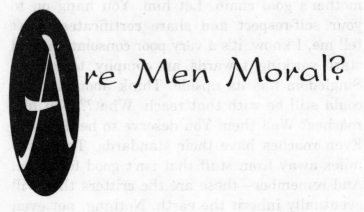

Are Men Moral?

All men are unfailingly faithful—till they discover the unadulterated joys of adultery. But that's okay—they don't see it as a moral issue. The reason men cheat on their wives is because the wives ask for it.

Men will go purple in the face saying they don't wish to be unfaithful. They don't want to be untrue. But what can they do if the woman in their life pushes them into it? It's all her fault. Everything is her fault. The justifications they trot out are many and varied. Men who find it impossible to stay monogamous claim it has a lot to do with their genetic wiring over which they have absolutely no control. They are *born* to be bastards. God *made* them that way.

They really cannot help it. Just like a dog cannot help salivating at the sight of a juicy bone. They insist their intentions are pure and noble when they fall in love. It is women who lead them astray—either the person they're involved with who fails to understand their impulses or the woman who drags them screaming and kicking into her boudoir, there to pull down their pants and get on with the job.

Most men believe deeply in this bilge. They aren't pretending. And they aren't fooling themselves either. So they say. Since the whole 'blame' falls on the woman anyway, they bear no responsibility in the matter.

Women who stray are called assorted charming names. 'Bitch' is one of them. Then there are 'slut', 'whore', 'nympho' and 'chaalu'. Men who do the same become heroes to their less adventurous contemporaries. They are dubbed 'studs' and other men whisper admiringly when they swagger into a bar to order a 'chhota'.

Fine. Nobody complains or cares because it is one of the 'eternal truths': Men screw around. Women weep.

Nobody wants to challenge this for it would be as futile as challenging the theory of relativity. Or Darwinism. In fact, Darwin should studiously be left out of this, since his study endorses all that women fear and don't wish to know, which is: men are lowdown, sneaky, sons of bitches when it comes to love and commitment because

Mother Nature intended it to be that way. (The use of the word mother is very significant in this context. It immediately establishes the gender of the original culprit.)

Intelligent women rarely get into pointless discussions in this area. They know it's a waste of time. Just as they know they will be blamed for everything and anything at the end of the discussion, given the original premise: women lead men into immoral conduct. Sure they do. They drag them by the scruffs of their necks and fling them into bed with another woman. Why would they do this? Because women are basically masochistic creatures who like nothing better than to feel intensely sorry for themselves and weep copious tears. Crying is really what turns them on. And in order to get turned on, they need to feel awful about their lives, themselves. What better way than to orchestrate an affair for the man they love? The ultimate torture and punishment? How can a woman possibly feel worse about herself than when her man is cheating on her—and she is responsible?

Since men are convinced it's self-degradation that makes a woman feel good about herself, they very magnanimously decide to cooperate by sleeping with her best friend. They are doing it for her sake—get it? So that she feels terrific as she awakes each morning with swollen eyes and a thick tongue. That is what she *wants* whether she realizes it or not. Anything else will make her feel lousy and rotten about her role in the man's life. She will believe she has failed and as we know nothing ruins a marriage/relationship more than a woman who sees herself as a failure.

Sadly, a lot of women connect with this tripe and brainwash themselves into accepting it when the man trots it out as an excuse for straying. The first stage involves anger. The next, defeat. Men, the swines that they are, capitalize on this swiftly. An extra-marital affair follows a familiar trajectory that doesn't vary too much, even when there are major cultural differences involved. Men go off to deposit their sperm in a woman not their committed partner and then they come home to gloat about it. The partner is supposed to understand and appreciate the fact that he has done it specially for her—so that she doesn't feel cheated in the marriage sweepstakes. If the woman refuses to react in the manner she is supposed to . . . say, she stares coldly at the goat and flips through a fashion magazine before embarking on a toe-painting exercise, the man feels let down and furious. He is there to see tears and hysteria. How dare she shortchange him in that supreme satisfaction? What is the point in having an affair if nobody gets hurt?

Men have peculiar views on the subject of affairs—what's good for the gander is not good for the goose. The goose is to stay home, honk but not bonk. And the justification for these lopsided double standards—as well as the answer to questions about his adulterous ways—is invariably the same: 'Don't blame me. I had nothing to do with it.' (Note: 'it' not 'her'.)

It's no use asking, 'So what the fuck were you up to anyway?' The man's answer ought to be 'I was . . . well . . . fucking . . . if you really must know.' He doesn't say that, of course, since he lacks the *savoir-faire* for straight talking. He also lacks a sense of humour under the circumstances—which is just as well since most women wouldn't see the joke anyway.

Veterans who have lived through the Adultery War say it's better to play ostrich and pretend you don't know a thing. The man who isn't confronted or pushed generally comes right back to the marital bed, with his tail between his legs. If you have a well-aimed kick in mind, this is the time to deliver it—after making sure he isn't protecting his genitals with an athletic guard. If, instead, you prefer to deliver your well-rehearsed 'quality of mercy' speech, go right ahead. He won't be impressed. And he isn't likely to change. Shaming a man into doing anything—even like changing his stinky underwear—is a complete waste of time for the simple reason that men hate being shamed. Trust me. A kick is more effective.

After that, there are two options. You may kick him right out of your life, or accept him for what he is—a son of a bitch—and treat him as such. The second option is far tougher but women who've taken it say it works provided there is some level of consistency.

Once a turd, always a turd. That is the basic truth about life. A turd cannot turn into a crunchy turnip. Neither can a turd ever smell of roses. Only a foolish woman can live with such a hope. And drive herself barmy in the bargain. Lecturing the chap is useless. Men wear invisible ear-plugs and don't hear a thing they wish to block out. Dragging children into an adult mess is counter-productive as well since men don't really see it as a moral issue in the first place.

'I stray. Therefore I am,' is how they regard their philandering. Besides, it is the 'other woman' who has done the seducing—even if the man has been lusting after her in public and private for years. Women who try and pal up with the bitch do so at their own risk. (Broads who sleep with other women's husbands rarely have what may be called finer instincts. They don't wish to know the wife, or connect with her pain. Heck—that wasn't the deal in the first place.) Those who've tried that route say it is humiliating and self-defeating. You bet. If you want to end up feeling as crushed and dry as sugar cane that's been put through a rusty wringer, go for this.

And remember, if the husband finds out you've been plaguing his lady love with phone-calls, letters, chocolates, flowers, sarees or jewellery, he will kill you. During the heat of his liaison it is the bitch who counts, not you. You, my dear, are the hand towel in the loo on which he wipes his greasy paws after gorging on a huge meal prepared by you in the hope that his stomach will influence his brain and make him see reason.

Rubbish.

While entangled in an affair, a man will happily starve, lose money, hair, weight and social standing because his groin is doing all the thinking. If his loins stay hot enough, he doesn't care about the rest of his body. He forgets hunger (of the food variety), thirst (I include his favourite Scotch), fatigue and even his memory ('What do you mean, where was I last night? I was at home, dammit').

Drop it. Leave it at that. Do not confront him with 'evidence' because in that state he is likely to accuse you of cooking it all up. Don't be surprised if he tries also to convince you, your family and friends that you are in the throes of some typical female problem. Those bloody hormones again. He might say you suffer from permanent PMS. That you are prematurely menopausal. That you've been taking mind-altering medication. That paranoia runs in your family. That your mother has put you upto it because she has always hated him. That your gynae had once told him that your 'female thing' was malfunctioning. That heavy periods had affected your brain. That someone had cast an evil spell on you out of sheer jealousy. Hardcore, irrefutable evidence is worth gathering only if you're planning to nail him for adultery in a bitter divorce suit and take his ass. If not, it's a complete waste of time and energy.

Sit it out, girl, if the marriage/relationship means anything at all to you. Laugh at his pathetic state. Sympathize with his sorry condition. And at all times appear friendly and receptive. Feed the fool when he's hungry. Give him a shoulder to cry on when the bitch spurns him. Pretend you can't read the clock when he rolls home at dawn. Take no notice of changed behaviour patterns ('Breakfast, what breakfast? I hate breakfast, you know that') and carry on leading a productive, cheerful life. Sooner than you think, he'll come crawling—and if the kick, discussed earlier, isn't on your agenda, make ample place for him on the bed and stay mum. This isn't the time to gloat or say something stupid like. 'I told you so. Everybody knows she's a bitch. See . . . if you'd only listened to me. Now look where you've landed. Everybody will be laughing at you. My God. I'd better stop going to the club for a couple of months. I can't possibly face all those women. Now stop sniffling and switch off the lights.' That isn't a smart way to handle the idiot by your side.

A clever gal will go fix the bounder a large drink, organize a serving of his favourite pakoras, put on some soothing music and talk about the glorious weather even if there is a storm raging outside. Kill the guy with kindness. It is, frankly, the only weapon you've got. Nothing will make him squirm more than a cheerful smile and complete silence on your part. Let him stew in his own juice. Men, like most other primates with small brains, are creatures of habit. They like familiarity. Comfort. Rubber chappals, torn pajamas, plastic mugs, frayed shoes. The bitch can give them everything—but where would she be able to lay her hands on the kurta-with-a-hole that the man loves so much that he has fought with the dhobi and you for darning it? Get the picture?

And for heaven's sake do not lecture to the broken, wounded, limping, whipped animal that has crept home after a battering. Because this same animal will somehow find the strength (perhaps that night itself) to creep right out, even if it means sleeping under the staircase and being mocked by the durwans. Men have amazing notions about their sense of dignity. When the bitch kicks them out of her perfumed bed, they want to climb into their own with their head held high. Let them. You know and they know who the sucker really is. So long as the score remains equal in terms of pride lost and pride retrieved, there is some hope for a future together—assuming that is what you still want. Women who idiotically deliver a sermon on moral rearmament end up like rotten turnips in the garbage pail.

Morality is tricky. Men genuinely believe there are two varieties of it—his and hers. They're puzzled when the in-built hypocrisy of such an attitude is pointed out to them. Double standards? Heck—yes. Isn't that how it should be? How it, in fact, is? Has always been? Will be forever? Reluctantly and shamefacedly, it has to be conceded that, bloody hell, that is so.

But there is a change in the offing, if you look hard enough. Traditional doormats are rapidly changing into contemporary blood-suckers—just as well. They are playing the game with reversed roles—and winning. Well . . . if one can talk of 'wins' in the first place.

A fortyish, divorced professor from an obscure American university, on a recent visit back home, was astonished to find innumerable predatory females stalking him. 'Mumbai spins on infidelity,' he informed everybody in triumphant tones, adding, 'I've been propositioned thrice in four days by married ladies looking for a quiet little 'nookie' on the side. 'Gals just wanna have fun,' was not explanation enough. The man wanted to conduct a sociological study to better understand the phenomenon.

It's reflected in movies and daily soaps as well—the unfaithful wife/girlfriend no longer has to pay for her adventures with her life. The very image of a female role model has undergone a change, with aggression not submissiveness being viewed as a desirable attribute. Today's young men prefer partners who pay their own bills and pick their lovers at random—the way men have always operated.

Is this new equation working? It's still too early to say. But women certainly are sleeping around much more and not suffering majorly from guilt. Some men find that most inconvenient—especially if the frisky lady happens to 'belong' to them. While they eye the women in their offices and joke about their beddability-quotient, they still expect the little woman back home to be engaged in activities that do not go beyond peeling potatoes, polishing brassware and making all the important decisions such as whether to invest in a spin-dryer or buy Munna his two-in-one instead.

No. Man, the Immoral Animal, is still not on the list of endangered species. He's free to run around and hunt for prey in the continued confidence of not getting caught himself—not really. The Moral Age is a long way off for men. In this one, only women are expected to have a conscience—and a clean nose.

Is It Possible To Actually Love A Man?

As Margaret Thatcher said so eloquently to David Frost: 'No. No. No. Women cannot love men.' They may pity them. Fear them. Adore them. Loathe them. Mock them. Envy them. But love? Impossible. Men are singularly unloveable creatures. It's easier to love dogs, for example, or exotic plants, or servants, or a favourite kitchen gadget. Curtains and linen too. But not men.

The reason is simple—women cannot understand what goes on in a man's mind, simple as it is. The thinking is different. When women talk about apples, men hear pears. It's not possible to have a straight conversation with a man even after living with him for forty years. We use a different language, us girls. Men don't quite get it. As for their communication skills, after co-habitating with their men for even a year, women rapidly learn to ignore the words and pay attention only to the signals. As we know by now, men make themselves understood in several different ways—like children. Or the young of animals. Their needs are pretty basic too—food, drink, sex. They aren't in the least bit interested in what a woman has to say, unless it is 'no' when the man is asking to bed her.

Wives who assume their spouses are paying close attention to what they're babbling about, assume wrong. Most men have a little button inside their heads which they switch off the moment they recognize the signs of an impending conversation. Men dread these moments. And would do anything to avoid them: leave town, feign appendicitis, fake a cardiac arrest, announce an uncontrollable urge to empty their bowels or, worst of all, start a counter-conversation simultaneously.

'Darling . . . the maid walked out on me just as Munni was howling from the potty. Not that I want to load you with servant trouble . . . but it is so bloody inconvenient. I had to kiss my kitty party goodbye and wash the baby's bum.

What else could I do? I mean . . . the outrage!
Bloody bitch. I'd given her all my old 'Garden'
sarees, and jeans too. Tchch. Of course she wore
jeans. Only on Sundays. I'd made that very
clear—no jeans on weekdays. What do you
mean you never noticed the jeans? How could
you anyway? We never see you on Sundays.
Come off it. You know that's true. Not that I'm
complaining or anything. It's fine with me. Golf
comes first. It always has. And beer with the
boys at the Gymkhana. No, I'm not looking for
a fight. Why are you saying that? Have I raised
my voice? Am I angry? Well, yes, I am. But not
at you. It's the bloody maid—yes, I'm on the
lookout for another one. This time, no sarees.
No jeans. I'll have to pay her more than we paid
this one. Which is why I brought this up in the
first place. It's okay by you, isn't it? Don't glare.
It wasn't my fault. Errr . . . we'll have to go to
the club for dinner. Naturally I couldn't cook.
Dammit, I could barely think. I was so upset—
where's the question of cooking? How would you
understand? Didn't expect you to either. It's all
very well for men to go to their stupid offices,
make a few phone calls, pretend to be working
and then come home and take out their
frustrations on the wife. Try staying home even
for three straight days and handling servant
problems. You'll go crazy—that's what. Okay,
okay. Call me a nag. It's the easiest thing to call
a woman. What? Did you say "Shut up"? You

actually asked me to shut up? Well fine, I'll shut up. Remember, my voice will haunt you when I'm dead and gone. And that could be very soon the rate we're going. And that's when you'll miss me. Come on, Munni, let's go to Nani's. At least we'll get something to eat there. Papa's dinner? Let him order a pizza over the phone.'

Foolishly, we live with the guy anyway. Why? Because we are afraid to live on our own. God (via our parents) has taught us to be so. We have been told we cannot survive by ourselves. That it's immoral. Unnatural. Freakish. Weird. That we *need* a man in our lives. Utter crap. But what the hell—they *are* fun to have around. They smell funny, act funny, talk funny, sleep funny, eat funny, think funny. That's the good part. They provide endless entertainment. We put up with them because they make us laugh. The crying part is not in this book, so we'll pretend it doesn't exist.

Mothers are on the side of men. They must be since they're forever pushing their daughters into hitching up with the first fellow who strolls up with a decent bank balance and a cute smile. Young girls trust their mothers and start believing there is no future for them unless there is a husband in it. Girls press panic-buttons by the time they're twenty-five and start getting touchy about their manless existence. It's difficult to convince a breathless bride-in-waiting that she doesn't have to go into hiding if she's single at twenty-six . . . or thirty . . . or forty-two. Once having bought the theory that there is no hope without a husband to call one's own, women automatically fall into line. And that's when they force themselves to accept hairy, smelly creatures in their beds and bathrooms. After a point, they get accustomed to a male presence and start missing the smell, touch and sound of 'maleness'. This is the state that is mistakenly identified as 'love'. But is it love? Try asking the advocates of it. 'When my husband leaves town on business, I stop cooking hot meals. I can't bear to eat his favourite dishes without him.' So . . . does the woman starve? No, she goes over to the neighbours' and has hot meals with *them*—with *her* favourite dishes, for a change.

'I love sniffing my husbands shirts after he's left the house. They remind me of him . . . his special smell.' The woman is generally checking whether or not to send the offending garment off to the laundry. And buy some fresh after-shave and cologne. Will she admit it? Never. 'I maintain a punishing fast during one month of the year—only fruit and milk. It is to ensure a long life for my husband.' Yeah, sure. And to keep up with the diet of the nauseatingly slim ladies at the aerobics class. 'My husband cannot bear to travel without me. He takes me on all his trips, even if he's going for just four days.' Naturally, someone's got to wash his undies and socks. Plus, butter his toast and smile at the bosses. 'He's really, really nuts about me. My God, he phones me from the office at least ten times a day. I have to keep my cellular phone switched on round the clock.' What on earth have you been up to and with whom? Is your man a detective or something? Doesn't he have work to do at his office? Sounds like a spy to me. 'God! My boyfriend is so jealous, so jealous, he doesn't allow me to even speak to another guy . . . forget dancing with someone else.' He sounds like an insecure, dictatorial jerk. Get out of it *now* and save yourself. 'My husband feeds me gulab-jamuns with his own hands everyday. I want to lose weight but he says he loves me the way I am.' Bullshit. The guy wants you to resemble an overfed cow so that nobody else gets attracted. Refuse to eat his proferred sweetmeats or—better still—stuff them right down his throat.

Women desperately want to believe in love, even though it's in an abstract sort of way. Without love, life loses its meaning and motivation. They want to believe in it so desperately, they'll love anyone or anything— even the world's worst creep, a habitual wife-beater, a Scrooge or an abusive s.o.b. They can't help themselves. They don't want to stand out in a world teeming with love-sick ladies. They want to conform and be one of the girls. They want a man to hang on to.

Men realize this soon enough. And use it to their advantage. They learn to manipulate their women without even trying. Most women actively want to be manipulated since they think that's the 'normal' way to be. They also confuse it with love ('Why would he bother to manipulate me if he didn't love me?').

It works both ways. Women manipulate men too (sorry—it had to be stated). So long as this tug-of-war remains at a manageable level, the marriage endures. It's when manipulation gets out of hand that conflict starts. Sweet-tempered ladies will tell you they cannot think of an existence without their mates. It's a little like someone saying they cannot visualize a life without an in-grown toenail. To these women, one says a soft, barely audible, 'Good luck'. They deserve whatever happiness they can snatch. Besides, they don't know any better. Simple people are happy enough with simple options. Marriage being just one of them. Ask them what they like about their man and they'll say simply, 'Just the fact that he's there.'

Okay, on this level, men are tolerable— even likeable. Take it further and we run into problems, like and love being two distinct slots. One can like a poem, or a movie, or Ruby Bhatia, or Akshay Kumar, or a double scoop of Minty Madness. Love? Women love their children, their fathers (rarely their mothers), their teachers, their pets, their face creams, their hair products, their jewellery, their silks, their bras, their letters. Stuff like that. Men—the bland types—like everything and everyone in an indiscriminate sort of way. Their love they reserve for frayed socks, stamp collections, old slippers, cricket bats, dated ties, T-shirts five sizes too tight for them, broken pocket combs, stained kerchiefs, credit cards, cars and music systems. Sometimes, they keep a little love aside for women—but it's always conditional. Plus, the threat of instant withdrawal remains.

Only fools love women unconditionally. Men with low intelligence and high ideals. Men who don't know any better. These are the guys who die of love pining for some undeserving wretch. The types who write poetry and drink themselves silly mooning over a maiden who at that very moment may be in bed with another man. Smart guys recognize at least one of life's bitter truths—women are selfish. Fickle too. To love them hopelessly is to leave yourself open to hurt and pain. Smart guys also believe in another awful truth: bed partners should stay in bed and not become business partners . . . unless the guy wants to be screwed literally *and* figuratively. And which guy does?

Despite their obvious shortcomings and failings, men are like teddy bears—great to cuddle on a monsoon evening. Loveable, yes, when their vulnerability stands exposed and they arouse the mother in you. Since love itself is so bloody irrational—who can explain why women 'love' men? Maybe, just maybe, it's because they are adorably stupid, most of them. Raw machismo is rather touching because it is so transparently innocent. Only an absolute 'duh' will fool himself into believing that it's his big, bad muscles we girls are in awe of and addicted to. We girls haven't stopped giggling since the first caveman clubbed a wild animal and dragged it back to impress his woman. He thought she was staring at his biceps. He was wrong. She was only looking at her next few meals.

Men In Love

ove hits men like a sharp slap in the face. The good news or the bad (depending on how you look at it) is that men in love are far more emotional, vulnerable and sincere than women in an identical state. How so? Men become defenceless and goofy when it comes to matters of the heart. They lose their rationality completely—even the toughest of them—and turn to mush. Some conceal their condition more successfully . . . but press the right buttons and bingo—it will all come pouring out.

Men in love are awfully sweet. Like eager puppies dying to be petted. Especially when love hits them in their late forties and fifties. That's when they behave like absolute chumps and don't seem to care whether the world knows it. They yap around looking and behaving like lost Dalmations. And they can't stop talking about the object of their passion—quite often an uninspiring cow with sad eyes and mousy hair. Is that how the man-in-love sees her? No. He sees Noorjehan bathed in moonlight. A naked Aphrodite. A Manisha Koirala swathed in silk. She is the most beautiful woman in the world to him and he doesn't care that everybody is laughing.

People are cruel. They shouldn't mock a man in love. They should sympathize. He cuts a pretty sorry figure while he goes on and on about his incomparable love when all he's doing in chasing a piece of tail. Men tend to confuse love and sex. They operate on a far more instinctual level than women, in this area. What they mistake for love isn't even lust, it is an uncontrollable urge to get into that particular woman's pants. Confront a man with this and he'll deny it vehemently. He will pretend to be deeply insulted. 'I'm not that kind of a person, I'll have you know,' he will say, or 'Speak for yourself,' he might add. But it's true.

People who have monitored such a dumb condition say it has something to do with chemicals and smells. Who knows? In any case, how do you tell a mooney-eyed fellow it isn't love but a chemical reaction he's experiencing? So you keep quiet and watch him make a total idiot of himself while all along you are thinking, 'Poor chap . . . should I let him cling to his illusions for just a while longer? Or should I break it to him that his condition is down right embarrassing to those in his immediate vicinity if not disgraceful to himself? Of course, some women find all this 'cho chweet' and immediately start treating the man-in-love like they would a pregnant bitch. Their eyes moisten and their voices alter as they pat a place by their side and urge him to park himself there, 'Tell all. Who is she? When are you going to make it official?' These are silly questions. They should be asking more pertinent ones like, 'Does she know you exist? Have you slept with her yet? Can you see yourself sleeping with her ten years down the line? Is her bum covered with blackheads? Have you checked her gums for pus? Does she have ingrown toenails?'

Nobody but nobody asks stuff like that. They waste time sweetly demanding to know, 'Is she from a good family? Have you told your parents yet? I hope she's got a good job—you know how important it is these days for a woman to work. Don't you just love her hair?' The last after scrutinizing her picture with its smudged image and curled-at-the-corners appearance. The man-in-love will beam and supply all the relevant info with the coy air of a virgin bride submitting herself to a gynae's intrusive interrogation.

Men-in-love are tiresome in the extreme since

they assume everybody they meet is as fascinated by their woman as they themselves are. 'I was just talking to her on the cell-phone, man,' the chap might say, 'I tell you . . . her voice turns me on. All I need is to hear her say, "Hello Raj", and I die.' Go die then, you want to say. Instead you look indulgently at him and add, 'I know just how you feel. Love is such a funny thing.' If you're in an excessively communicative mood you carry on like an idiot yourself. 'I remember when I first met that creep I later married . . .' The truth is nobody cares about them or their love. Men, being basically dumb, don't understand indifference or even recognize it. They sicken friends and family with gooey, mushy stories that are generally so pedestrian they don't even ring true. Also, it rarely occurs to them that they may just be cruising down a one-way street to nowhere, love being the biggest bum trip in the world.

The older they are, the harder they fall. If the love-object is half their age, they are goners from the word go. While the shrewd little hot number flatters their ego by tap-dancing in public, her eyes survey the scene for potential bed-mates. The old man's darling is really a greedy, smart strumpet who has him where she wants him—at her feet where he stays till he dies, leaving her all the lolly. Old men in love are even more irrational than regular chaps in their twenties and thirties—naturally so. They've been given a second (third? fourth? fifth?) chance and they don't want to blow it. They also know the world is looking on and laughing. They have a point to prove. Producing a child becomes priority number one—look at Anthony Quinn, Picasso, Francois Mitterand, Laloo Prasad Yadav. They are telling us something—that the old equipment is well-oiled and in working order, thank you. The woman has nothing to lose and everything to gain. If the marriage fails, the reasons for its failure will be obvious enough—him. 'Poor woman. How could she bear to live with that bag of bones?' Because of his bags of money, dearie. 'Yes . . . but you can't sleep with dollars/dirhams/yen/rupees.' That's true. But did you see her chauffeur/cook/butler/personal trainer/spiritual guru/raakhi brother? 'Like that, huh?' What did you think? Celibacy wasn't part of the deal.

Funny how people always assume men marry for sex and women for money. They're right, of course. Love rarely figures in the matter. Right, there too. Men overrate love. Women place it in the proper context. It comes below home and security, marble flooring, dog-walkers, life insurance policies, two vacations annually, a no-dandruff clause and separate bathrooms, which is why women rarely write rhapsodically about love in all its glory. They don't build mausoleums like the Taj Mahal to perpetuate the memory of a dearly beloved even if they can afford to finance the bloody thing independently. They don't write sonnets à la Shakespeare or even soppy books that elevate love. Their stories are generally about loss and regret even when they do involve love (*Gone with the Wind*) and the height of romance includes a broken heart (broken bones too, sometimes). Women are incapable of celebrating love with the same kind of innocence as men. They analyse it too much. Read a lot into what is a very simple, basic emotion. And finally kill the feeling by adding a generous dollop of suffering to it. Women have to suffer in order to feel good. They suspect anything that doesn't involve sacrifice and pain. If love comes their way easily, they reject it as being superficial. Even fraudulent. Many test love like they test the purity of gold or the clarity of a diamond.

Men don't. They are naive enough to accept love at face value . . . till reality hits or bites them. Often they go through life believing in their version of love. Lucky them. They're happier for it. Like simpletons are fortunate because their brains are incapable of grasping life's complexities. Absolutely so. Men are simpletons when they fall in love. Women are quick to capitalize on this. Just as well. Good marriages aren't about love. They're about deals. So long as the profit-sharing is on a reasonably fair basis, nobody complains. The minute the balance sheet begins to look wonky, the deal is called off. This may not happen on paper and remain at an unspoken, unacknowledged level, but happen it does. One party withdraws co-operation and support. The other carries on valiantly till either death or divorce settles the question.

Men are slower to recognize the absence of love, or maybe women are smarter at pretending it exists well after its disapperance. Either way, men lose out. They cling on to a feeling, because it is the feeling they crave . . . not necessarily the woman. In order to sustain that feeling they're prepared to go to great and absurd lengths. Suicide being just one of them. The mushiest poetry is written by men. The mushiest songs sung by them. Suckers.

Thank God for that, though. Imagine if they were to be as hard-hearted, cold-blooded and calculating as women. Even the most ruthless of men crumble when love hits them (Hitler comes to mind). One rarely hears about power-ladies giving it all up for the love of a telephone operator or postman. Which is why the Duke of Windsor is so tragic and so comic. He gave up his kingdom for a woman who, reportedly, gave him nothing more significant than a very competent b.j. in return. The story sucks.

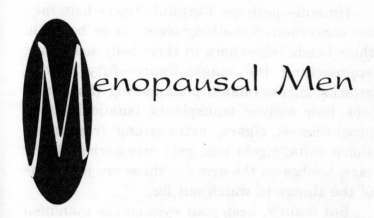

Menopausal Men

Look around random swimming pools anywhere in the world. You'll spot 'em. They're the chaps wearing the slinky, high-cut skinwear, all-over tans and goofy expressions. And they're strutting their stuff pretty brazenly. Average age—forty-five to fifty.

But they do come younger, too. Like the tennis player who did so much for the lowly, ungainly, almost ugly, garden-variety jock strap—Thomas Muster. He acts and looks menopausal even if he isn't anywhere close to the age when 'the change' happens. It's far too much of a cliché to say male menopause has nothing to do with hormones, raging or quietly slipping into a coma. It is more a state of mind.

Hmmm—perhaps. Certainly true where men are concerned. Something seems to go 'boing' in their heads (elsewhere in their body too) while approaching the magic figure—fifty. Panic-attacks. Stress-related philandering (ha!), nose jobs, hair weaves, transplants, fanatical fitness programmes, cigars, extra-strong fragrances, sharp suits, gigolo ties, gold accessories, flashy cars, bimbos on the arm . . . these are just some of the things to watch out for.

But mainly, keep your eyes on the man/men wearing the hottest swimming trunks at resorts. Those are the ones. And monitor their progress around the pool. While other vacationers arrive in holiday gear and then strip down to thongs, these fellows lounge around the property round-the-clock clad in day-glo monokinis, gut sucked in, chest stuck out, eyes hungry and that unmistakable swagger as they crook a finger in the direction of the bartender to order a mid-afternoon highball. Notice also, the crow's feet around the eyes, the nervous tic, the quick fluffing out of thinning hair, the nonchalance with which a smooth dive into the cool waters is attempted (often botched up too). If you at all feel like it, make eye contact and wait. Minutes later the M.M. (menopausal male) will be by your side asking, 'Drink?' If you smoke, the lighter will be whipped out of nowhere at an astonishing speed while maintaining a steady eyeball-to-eyeball gaze through the ritual.

Indicate the deckchair closest to your own and blow smoke in a neutral direction. Within minutes, the M.M. will be throwing you his well-rehearsed, rather shopworn chat-up line while looking over the top of your head at the nubile sixteen-year-old floating by on an oversized plastic duck.

Welcome to the world of M.M.s.

Insecurities be damned, M.M.s tend to climb onto everybody's nerves with their studied, icky charm and cocky manner. They live in their failed pasts while dreaming about a glorious future—often in the Bahamas. There is a tragic quality to their longings.

Menopause seems to affect poets more strongly than others. There are at least two in Bombay who go around re-embellishing a mythical track record supposedly littered with conquests of the most unbelievable kind. Unable to deal with the present, nor prepared to cut off from the past, they live in a suspended state talking endlessly about their triumphant youth spent in various bars across the world bedding notorious call-girls. Nobody believes them. Worse—nobody is even listening to their schoolboyish bragging. Friends look away uncomfortably—others sympathize. It happens to men in their fifties, they mutter. Let's be kind. It would be so easy to behave cruelly and yell. 'Bull-shit.'

Somebody should do just that—especially

when these dried-up versifiers keep referring to their own genius and damn anybody else attempting to make a mark in the line. M.M.s are paranoid about (a) growing old; (b) growing impotent. They detest younger fellows and actively conspire to 'finish them off', without actually specifying how, where or when. Since they refuse to come to terms with age, they spend a good deal of time, money and energy fighting it. At work, they know they're seen as losers. If they haven't made it to the top of the heap by fifty—brother, they're out of the race. Professionally, there's little to look forward to— besides a retirement plan and a life insurance policy.

There's always golf, of course. But look around at any golf course and you'll see a green filled with scowling, frustrated men. If the professional front is fuzzy, the home front can't be much better. Men who perform in the boardroom generally do pretty well in the bedroom too. It has to do with drive and ambition. M.M.s do recognize at some level that it's more or less over for them—they've probably been superseded, left out in the cold and snubbed by colleagues half their age. It is time to discover new turf and prove themselves on it. What better than a golf course? Suddenly these non-motivated bounders become maniacs with clubs. They awake at the crack of dawn and set off determinedly to prove their macho-worth with other M.M. victims.

Weekends are devoted exclusively to working on the swing . . . along with networking with that chap who has interests in timber down south. Nothing like combining leisure with a little business on the side. That way, wifey back at home doesn't mind being left to her own devices (and the hunky driver) all that much either.

Doesn't she? Chances are, wifey is battling her own hormonal demons—and losing. She is getting chunkier, nastier and uglier. 'It's temporary, you asshole,' she snarls as yet another hot flush cripples her. 'Oh yeah?' he sneers as he packs his golf gear and prepares to push off. Wifey is in no mood to engage in well-modulated, couple-conversation. It's time for the M.M. to get his ass out of the house a.s.a.p. He does just that . . . yelling out to the wife to see her H.R.T. adviser—also a.s.a.p. Menopausal women have an edge over menopausal men—they can blame everything on wayward hormones. Hormones are the culprits. But the whole world knows that for men, there is no real alibi. Well, there is—failure. But no one wants to cite that.

M.M.s begin spending more and more time outside the home once they realize their wives are sailing in the same boat. Since hanging around at the office isn't as fulfilling or challenging as it used to be (how does one deal with a callow twenty-something hot-shot calling the shots?), the M.M. shifts the action to club bars . . . where he knocks back a few vodka tonics and discusses a mega contract he's about to sign. Drinking buddies cringe in embarrassment and order a fresh round. Not that the M.M. notices any of this—he is far too full of himself. He holds forth on grand schemes that are imminent, ambitious expansion plans, over-the-top projects, foreign collaborations . . . mega deals awaiting a nod from the right ministry. And all the while he is pushing up his shirt collar, running his fingers through the toupée/wig/weave and eyeing young daughters of friends he has grown up with.

He has sex and money on his mind. And that's where both will remain. He knows that. The world knows that. It's okay. The man has problems. He wants to stay youthful forever. He wants sex—lots of it. Also, forever. He also wants a six-pack gut, thick, dark hair, no wrinkles . . . and male equipment that works at one-hundred-per-cent efficiency level on demand, every single time—no glitches. Fair enough. The man's requirements are modest. Even if he is totally mad.

The

Portable

Man

Men In Bed

Most women will admit that they vastly prefer soft fluffy, lacy pillows to hairy, smelly, lazy partners who snore. Women who've savoured life and been around will also tell you that the secret of their successful love lives has been separate bedrooms and more importantly, separate bathrooms.

Psychologists mislead people into believing that couples who sleep together, stay together. Not so, say the couples themselves. All-night cuddles end at the honeymoon cottage—and just as well. Women are like cats in this respect. They value their privacy and individuality. Just as cats cannot be persuaded to grace your lap (unless it is the cat who's looking for a little warmth) women too dislike being used as bolsters once the business of sex is over.

Fortunately, most sensible men feel the same way too and promptly turn over and go to sleep after remembering their early-morning game of golf. This is fine by women. Really. It is a myth to suggest women need post-orgasmic hugs and kisses. They don't. They prefer a good book, but will settle for a lousy TV movie in its place if they have to.

The act of sex should not be confused with the act of love, which is more complicated and harder to decode. Sex is functional, no matter what the experts tell you. If both partners regard it as such, the question of incompatibility doesn't arise. Good sex is based on recognizing mutual signals and following them through. Bad sex, unfortunately, is what defines a majority of relationships. A woman must identify the basic difference between what sex means to men and what she means when she says she wants it. Men will lie about this (but then, men will lie about anything)—their idea of perfect sex is programmed sex minus any frills. The unsexiest aspect of a relationship for them is the responsibility that goes with it. Sex with a price-tag is the world's yuckiest bargain—unless you are a man who likes to pay for his pleasure. Women, on the other hand, use sex as a bargaining chip all the time, even if they aren't consciously aware of doing so.

A sulking wife, for example, withholds sexual

favours till the husband comes crawling contritely to her. Wives also refuse to play ball unless some promise is kept—a promise the husband rarely remembers having made in the first place. But such is the ferocious power of the male urge, he is likely to pledge his life, his share certificates, his farm house, his mother's diamonds, anything at all, provided she lets him in. This is the crucial moment, girls—lose it and live to regret your loss forever. The stupidest word to use at this point is 'later'. There *is* no later. There is only 'now'. Keep a fountain pen handy just in case important documents need to be signed before you ummm . . . oblige. Once the man has gained entry—forget it. Instant amnesia generally follows. What shares? What diamonds? What promises? Timing is all.

Men say they can't stand women who play hard-to-get. Not true. Non-availability is very attractive provided the potential endures. Nothing fires up a fellow as much as fantasy. He likes the thought of a conquest more than the conquest itself. A 'material girl' senses this and plays the waiting game with panache. Alas, a poor wife rarely has a choice. She speaks, not from a position of strength but abject dependence (well, in most cases).

Saying 'no' too frequently has its own pitfalls, though. Chances are the man will wander off to find himself a more accommodating bed partner. But saying 'yes', when you actively want to scream 'no', is even worse—unless the man is drunk out of his mind (in which case, he won't be anywhere close to his target anyway). Never strike boudoir deals with a drunk—you'll always end up short-changed.

Men behave peculiarly in bed and women must recognize individual behaviour patterns if only for their own survival. It sounds like a cliché, but as in the origins of most clichés, there is an element of truth here too. Men equate the bed with a battlefield where victory means everything. Men behave like warriors (oh well—G.I. Joes then) when they climb out of their underwear and prepare themselves for the combat ahead. Women find their expressions and gestures very comical—which is why so many women keep their eyes closed (it's unsexy to giggle when a guy is on the hop.)

Unless the woman is playing aggressor, she'll probably be prone while the man looms over her. Even if she lands on top later, she has to start off on her back. From this perspective most men look kinda odd, especially if they believe they are acrobats in addition to being accomplished warriors. Men who grunt, groan and get noisy in bed turn women off, which is also the reason why well-trained lover-girls adopt a counter-strategy and out-decibel their partners with a repertoire that includes banshee-like screams, moans and wails. All this is mistakenly assumed to be a spontaneous outpouring of passion. Forget it. The screams are designed to distract the man from things like small breasts, unshaven legs, fuzzy armpits, pitted thighs, ugly birthmarks, scabies, blind nipples, bad breath, b.o., smudged make-up, lice, scars and other such impediments to ecstasy. These are also the reasons why women generally prefer the lights to be off—they can't see the man looking comical and he can't see them looking unattractive.

Men, on the other hand, don't bother about anything else when they're horny. They want it—and they want it immediately, with or without full lights blazing. Sharon Stone (or at least as she projects herself in the movies) appreciates and understands this. That's what makes her the world's most desired woman. Unfortunately, for every Stone there are millions of wilted drooping flowers, over-anxious about their bodies, unsure about their performance. They need time, privacy and discretion. Men don't believe in stuff like that. It's heave-ho, in we go, before a woman can say 'Wait' or 'Stop'. In either case, those two words are a complete waste of time. No man waits or stops once the woman has taken her clothes off. Mike Tyson, for example, paid a huge price for coming to his own conclusions when the winner of a beauty contest consented to go up to his hotel room at an interesting hour, wearing interesting clothes. If women are foolish enough not to mean business when they disrobe, they deserve a man-in-a-hurry.

Do men suffer from similar anxieties? Hell, no. The unlikeliest of chaps tumble into bed imagining they're doing the woman a favour. Maybe their mirrors tell them a different story about themselves or they don't look into them. For if they did, they'd see some truly funny sights.

What makes guys good in bed? Ask a woman and she'll promptly use the dreaded 'F' word. No, not the obvious one—but 'foreplay'. Ask a man and his gaze will travel downwards as he boasts. 'Performance baby, performance.' Urge him to add a few more words. A couple of descriptive sentences. He'll merely reach for his cell-phone and conduct a meaningless conversation with someone—anyone. If you insist on probing further, you're unlikely to hear anything more illuminating than a series of incoherent mumbles. 'Performance . . . you know . . . like . . . like . . . performance?' Sure. It's best to leave it there—cryptic and to the point.

Fact is, *he doesn't know*. Or worse—he doesn't want to tell. Maybe the same question should be posed to women—experienced women. They will say there are two categories of men: a) good lovers. b) good husbands. No overlap. Or, rarely so. Good lovers (G.L.s) deliver the goods—that's their job. They're attentive, sensitive, appreciative—and hard. They aren't clumsy with female clothing. They never fumble with bra buckles. They always handle expensive sarees with reverence while undrèssing partners, love post-coital showers during which they dutifully soap unreachable areas and later pat the woman dry with fluffy towels. Some of them get paid for their services. Laid and paid. Which is perfect.

And we are only discussing frills and fluff here. Women are frequently foolish about both, preferring them to the 'real thing'—which by the way, rarely varies—the old missionary position, take it or leave it.

That leaves good husbands (G.H.s) who do all the paying but not necessarily the laying. *'Theek hai,'* say their mates while absently waiting for their quarterly humping session ('If it's March—we have to file our tax returns and remember to fuck, darling'). G.H.s who are also G.L.s generally have impressive, awesome wives-with-appetites. They cannot afford to screw up unless they wish to lose their trophies to a harder-working candidate—generally the chairman of the company.

Wives who read American sex manuals constantly complain that their men have never ever managed to hit the 'G'-spot . . . the one they've been assured definitely exists and can be located by an adept lover. Well, since most husbands prefer *The Economist* to paperbacks dealing with non-existent, mysterious spots hidden in their mates' crevices, the quest for the ultimate 'O' remains a frustratingly unsuccessful one . . . at least for the 'how-to' seekers of sexual bliss.

The other big grouse women harbour deals with the 'PPMA' syndrome—men who are 'Physically Present but Mentally Absent'. 'I like to copulate with my mind,' awakened ladies insist. But are the men listening? Nope. Their minds are otherwise engaged and in any case, they prefer to reserve them for issues more important than their wives' delicate tissues. Which is why the standard response from these unfullfilled ladies each time their hubbies wish to lie back and enjoy a lazy b.j. is: 'Go suck your own.'

Perhaps the time has come for men to start saying, 'Not tonight, darling. I have a headache.' Which will be the wife's cue to snap, 'If you don't watch it, buster, you are going to end up humping the dog.' Remember, there is no such thing as 'No'—especially in marriage.

If you can't make it—fake it.

For most women, marriage is a life-long lie. They are in it because their options (if any) are limited. It's marriage or wasteland.

Sex is always and only on a man's terms. If he can't get it up (fatigue, low sex-drive, lack of interest, another woman, another man—a combination of all the above), he can't get in . . . and you can't get it off. It's that simple. Men prefer sex on demand, with them doing all the demanding. A busy Bollywood actor confessed to a confidante that he was taken aback when his equally busy actress-wife often wanted 'it' right after he staggered home from the studios, dead beat and in need of a drinkie, not a quickie—the stiffest thing on his mind being a whisky and not the dingaloo.

Men can jig-jig anywhere and anytime—of their choosing, of course. First thing in the morning, last thing at night, depending entirely on how badly they want it. If they took a few seconds off to open those squeezed-shut eyes and study their partners' expressions while grunting and sweating over them, they'd be in for a rude surprise. Terry McMillan's *Waiting to Exhale* has two splendid demonstrations of men's total self-absorption while making love. The women lying under them make no attempt to disguise their disgust and revulsion but do the human pistons going in-out, in-out notice? No . . . they're far too preoccupied with their own ejaculation.

Yes, men are preoccupied with their genitals, but upto a point—the preoccupation does not stop them from hallucinating about their attractiveness to all women. And their expertise, of course. Clever ladies play along and make their puny men feel like Bengal tigers on the prowl. Actually, these very tigers turn into mewing pussycats once they're through with copulation. Post-coital behaviour varies widely of course, but even so, it is possible to predict a certain set of responses. Some men prefer to smoke thoughtfully while stroking the woman's arm in an absent-minded way. Others smoke and switch off moodily, sometimes taking a little time over their own bodies, maybe fiddling idly with their flaccid penises. Others turn their backs on their still-panting partners and begin snoring contentedly seconds after the last spasm. The worst kind reach for the remote even as the woman catches her breath. There are other options: newspapers, magazines, books, a quick shower, chewing gum, cognac—another frenzied round. Basically, men disengage and disconnect as quickly as they couple. It's all over within seconds—any other behaviour is a put-on designed to please the woman, provided they care sufficiently about her in the first place.

Where does that leave foreplay? Like I said, men display distinct before-and-after traits. Foreplay is not high on their priority list but they've read somewhere (probably on an airplane) that today's women expect it. They try and oblige but so grudgingly, it doesn't seem worth the bother. Women take a lot of time to warm up (it varies between twenty minutes to twenty years). However, to get them going is an important first step that most men would prefer to skip. While women sweetly say they aren't looking for an elaborate ritual (liars) it doesn't exactly hurt for the man to devote say, twelve seconds to kissing her, stroking her, fondling her and uttering a bagful of lies about love before actually unzipping his fly. Women are suckers for such stuff and start making silly gurgling noises at the back of their throats while the men stare anxiously at the bedside clock and wait for those interminable twelve seconds to finally end and leave them guilt-free to go about their original business—which is penetration, ejaculation, withdrawal.

Foreplay bores men. Anything that cuts into penetration-time bores them. Since foreplay has become an obligatory part of modern-day love-making, they go through the motions as if they had a gun held to their heads. Men aren't great kissers either (young boys, yes, but that's because they haven't discovered the main course yet). Women aren't crazy about men's mouths too—especially if they've recently puffed on a fat cigar or eaten pan-masala. If beer and biryani have also been thrown in, the kissing-wissing gets decidedly unappetizing . . . and the entire sexual menu is ruined. Men and women need an orientation course if kissing is to be an integral part of the kootchie-koo business. Tongue, no tongue. Open or closed mouth. Saliva or no saliva. There are several aesthetic factors involved and people tend to disregard them—at their own risk, naturally. Men who slobber and slaver all over women, covering their faces and bodies with sticky wetness, have to learn to restrain their spittle. Men who kiss through clenched teeth and firmly clamped jaws must be taught how to unwind. Men who don't know how to support a woman's neck and nearly break it while exploring her mouth, should have the same done to them. Men who attempt an Errol Flynn number without his rakish style, need a sharp kick between their legs.

But men who can melt a woman's reserve by holding her gracefully, running their fingers through her hair while their lips make music together, aah—such men deserve to be kissed back warmly and passionately with the head thrown back, hair tickling the waist, one foot off the ground, arm flung around a strong neck, back arched, eyes shut and mouth invitingly open—not too wide, not too pouting, open just enough to savour the pleasant flavour of the man's probing tongue.

If you're looking for still more explicit instructions, read any one of my novels. Or invest in the *Kama Sutra*.

We've dealt with foreplay, play and afterplay. But what really goes on in a man's mind during the act of love? Honest answer? Nothing at all. He has no mind during intercourse. Everything begins and ends at his genitals. More specifically on their functioning. The man cannot think beyond his erection. It fascinates him. Obsesses him. Thick enough? Long enough? Hard enough? Will it last?? It is the appearance and performance of his own organ that turns him on. After a point, the woman becomes irrelevant. It doesn't matter who or what she is. What does matter is how the little guy between his legs is doing. The best sex-stimulant in the world for a man is not a pair of enormous knockers, or even legs that start at the eyeballs. It's the sight of himself pumping away. Ask any stud. If he's even half-way truthful, he'll admit to it.

And then, go have yourself a little cry. A lot of women should feel relieved to read this—it means they don't have to go on killer-diets or worry excessively about their orange-peel thighs. The man they want to bed is only marginally interested in such details. What he wants is a piece of ass and he wants it now. More fool you if you're the sort to fog your fancy shades with self-doubt and anxiety concerning cellulite. Forget crepey skin and drooping breasts. Concentrate on getting the guy revved up. Once you've got him going, relax. His narcissism will take care of the rest.

Young brides feels awfully let down by male behaviour. They've taken the trouble to work on their bodies for months. They want their husbands to notice. To care. To compliment. They do that—while the honeymoon lasts. And even then, it's largely the auto pilot mechanism in their minds that takes over and plays the tape. What's on this soothing tape? Mainly meaningless, impersonal compliments that could as easily apply to any female of any species. Do not despair. Remind yourself that men have a limited repertoire in any language or culture. They don't know better. Take love lyrics. Has anybody improved substantially on say, Frank Sinatra's all-purpose, all-weather, 'The moon is blue and I love you' drivel?

Besides, it's foolhardy to confuse love, fondness, affection, charity, devotion, fear and sex. Men rarely want to have sex with women they respect or look up to. It seriously damages their egos. It also makes them feel awfully guilty and wretched about themselves. Remember too, men rarely 'make love'. They generally 'have sex'. Women equate the two and end up feeling very sorry for themselves. They crib about feeling used, being exploited, when what they really mean is that they haven't had an orgasm.

A great big earth-mover that is. There are millions of women out there who insist they don't know what that word means. Okay. You needn't know what it means. But you have a right to experience it. No? No, say the prim ones, primly. What you don't know, you don't miss. It's the same with dogs. Or so the vets say, when you ask whether to mate or not mate your pedigreed Great Dane. Don't even think of it, squawk some experts. Once the dog gets the scent of a bitch, you are in mucho trouble. He'll then want it all the time. 'It' as in coupling, not in scent. Certain cultures apply the same thinking to women. Sex for procreation, not pleasure, is an age-old dictum conspired to deny women the Big 'O'. But even in societies where they do know better, women complain that it's the men in their lives who are insensitive to what's going on *down* there, other than what they themselves are experiencing *in* there. So, why don't the women just holler out and demand what they are entitled to, for God's sake? Because it's unfeminine to do so, they simper. Too bad, in that case.

Do women actively and actually enjoy 'the act'? Are you serious? Given the choice between an unread bestseller, an unseen movie or a good girlie-gossip over a desultory, obligatory duty-fuck, most women would go for the former options. Sex is seen as both a bore and a chore. Practically anything else in life seems sexier in comparison—like a new perfume or a shampoo that smells of green apples. Alas, sex is one hundred per cent result-oriented for gals with an agenda—and who doesn't have one these days?—marriage, babies and/or a fat deposit in a Swiss account. What the hell is the point of all that heaving and grunting otherwise? It's different for guys—sex *is* the point, period.

Poor men. Very often, they believe a woman is just so delighted to have them inside her, it doesn't matter a jot that she's feeling nothing at all besides soreness and discomfort. They honestly believe it's an honour they've bestowed and that the woman ought to feel deeply grateful.

A lot of women encourage this delusion because it serves their purpose. The 'bigger' a man feels, the better he is to her. Through the centuries, courtesans have been trained to make men feel precisely that—bigger. In stature, size and self-esteem. A cunning woman instinctively knows that the way to a man's heart is via his penis. If she has, or pretends to have, good feelings about her man's organ, he will be her devoted slave for life. Remember, he is very sensitive about this part of his anatomy. He feels protective towards the little bugger. And defensive too. A woman who fondles and plays with it, coos over it, compliments it, even talks to it (addressing it, and not who it's attached to, directly) is the woman who will get her solitaires and gambling money without a murmur.

But there are enough guileless women who make their distaste known. A few rules to observe in case you happen to fall into this category. no matter what your personal feelings or reservations are, make sure you beam when he's strutting around showing off his erection. Never pull faces, frown, or stare suspiciously at it. If the man is naked in the room, don't take your eyes off it by watching television or reading. He'll take that as a personal insult. In case your hand strays in bed and comes into contact with a rapidly hardening extension of flesh, do not jump out of your skin like you've been electrocuted. Do not remove your hand or wipe it hastily. Do not slide purposefully to the outer edge of the bed. Do put down your book and smile fondly in its general direction. Do make an indulgent comment about its state. Do blow or bestow kisses like you would on an old friend or your neighbour's newborn. Do allow your fingers to linger while a smile plays on your lips. Do move closer to the 'object' and register its growing presence. Under *no* circumstances should you ignore or insult it. To do so would be to risk a major showdown that will be so structured as to make out it has nothing to do with your bad attitude. You'll probably be coldly reminded that you've forgotten to sew on his shirt buttons, keep fresh towels in the bathroom, make tomato chutney, change the bedside table lamp bulb, clip his ingrown toenail, order enough sodas for the party tomorrow night, switch the brand of toilet paper, summon the carpenter, call the dentist . . . stuff like that.

Even though most women find male genitals comical if not downright hateful, they instinctively learn to keep their feelings to themselves. Or share them with other like-minded women. Those who are insane enough to confide in a man find themselves out in the cold wondering where they'd failed. It wasn't your parathas, honey. Those were perfect. It was your lack of tact. Never mind. There's always a hard option and a soft one in life. Next time, go for the hard one, girl.

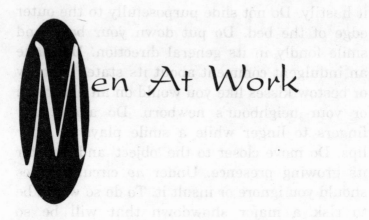

Men At Work

It is known. It has been issued as a statement. It is written in letters of pure gold: men do important work. And women? C'mon. Are you kidding? So what if you are the CEO of a blue-chip company? That's just something you do on the side. It isn't *real* work, you know. Real work is reserved for men. Yeah. *They* do it. God said so too. Which is why men come home and watch television. Put their feet up over the weekends. And hang around in their underclothes during off-hours. Men need to relax. Unwind. Cool off. Women don't. Because women don't do real work. The heavy stuff. They only run the house. Raise children. Handle finances. Contribute equally to the family kitty. Replace bulbs. Drive the car. Invest wisely. Cook. Clean up. Put up with pests. And yes, get to the office on time.

Big deal. Look at the men. My, my. Now, *these* are the guys who know what slog means. Watch any peon in a government office. The guy snoozing on a stool. The one refusing to carry a file from table A to table B. The other one taking his umpteenth tea break. They're all typical. Track any one of them to his home. That's right. He heads for the television set, after taking off his clothes and ordering tea. He is not to be disturbed, by anybody or anything. Least of all, children—even the one running an alarmingly high fever and begging for some water while mummy makes daddy his tea. The man barks out to his wife in the kitchen, 'Woman, your child needs water. Please fetch it quickly. I can't hear the news with the kid whimpering.' The woman lowers the gas under the milk pan lest the milk boil over and rushes to the child with water. The water spills, the child howls. The man roars, 'Can't I get some peace in this house? I come back after a hard day's work— and this is my reward?' The woman keeps shut. She dares not point out that she has put in exactly the same hours at her job. And that it's the second day of her period. She mutely picks up her sick child and flees. Note: a sick child automatically becomes 'hers'. A clever, well-behaved one is always 'his'.

Switch to Mr Tycoon as his Mercedes glides

into the portico. He strides into his luxury home with two minions carrying his briefcases behind him. He walks into his air-conditioned bedroom and takes off his clothes. He reaches for the remote control. He orders a drink. He throws the children out of the room. And smiles distantly at his harassed wife. She is allowed to remain in the room provided she tiptoes around the place and keeps her mouth shut. The tycoon is getting de-stressed. It's important for the peace of the house to leave him alone and look respectful. After all, he has come back after doing important work. And the wife? Oh . . . what the hell, she has done her duty as a wife, career person and mother—that's all. Why make a noise about it?

Women ask to be marginalized. And they deserve it too. Men rarely behave like martyrs. Women invariably do. Men take it for granted that the entire household is so structured as to make life more comfortable for them. Women cringe when it comes to indulging themselves even slightly. Men experience no guilt. Women, only guilt. Men command respect merely by being born men, women have serious self-doubts about their eligibility for a place in the human race.

Men are not expected to keep track of basic stuff like the number of children they've fathered. Legitimately, that is. Their children's names. Exact ages. Levels of education. Or birthdays. These are in mummy's department. And mummy is made to feel it is a privilege to be given this portfolio to handle on an exclusive basis. Sometimes men contribute to the process by actually turning up for a special occasion and taking interest in the proceedings. But it is an unwritten rule that they are exempt from the boring stuff. Parents' Day at school. College admissions. Dentists' appointments, minor surgeries, major emotional crises, interviews, and if they can possibly avoid it, weddings, too. When they do condescend to show up, everybody is expected to keel over with gratitude and show appreciation. Especially their wives who have in fact spent their entire lives waiting for the event and working towards it.

Men airily dismiss their occasional complaints by saying, 'All this is a woman's department. You handle it. Why should I meet the school principal anyway? Incidentally . . . who is he? What's the bloody fool's name? Does he think I've nothing better to do than cancel my meetings to see him?' Wives foolishly try and put the whole thing into perspective by pointing out that the principal is a woman. Not a man. And the child risks rustication if not expulsion for a serious offence. Does it make the slightest difference? Absolutely not. 'It's your problem. Handle it,' the man announces before walking out. So, what does the woman do? Obvious. She handles it.

If the child does get thrown out after all this,

the man turns his fury on her: 'All your fault. You must've botched the whole thing up. Our son has been expelled just because of you. How will I face the guys at the club? What am I going to say?' The woman squirms and promises to hush the whole thing up. 'Can't trust you with anything,' the man thunders as he packs his golf clubs and tries to phone the caddy at the club. The woman trails behind him looking apologetic. 'Don't worry, darling,' she pleads, 'I'll find an even better school. Or there is always Singapore. They take anybody there.' The man pokes his head out of the T-shirt he's getting into and sneers, 'Oh yeah? Singapore, huh? And who's going to pay for it?' The woman whispers timidly, 'I am. I've already paid the deposit.' The man glares at her menacingly. 'So . . . now you've started doing things behind my back, have you? Who gave you permission to make such a decision?' She stutters. 'But . . . but . . . I did try and bring it up with you several times. You kept saying, "Later, not now, I am busy." The last date was about to expire . . . so . . . I thought . . .' and she trails off while he slams his fist down and shouts, 'You thought, you thought. These days you are thinking too *much*. Now you want to ruin our son's life by sending him away. Let me tell you, if anything goes wrong, I won't be responsible, got that?' The woman nods. The man turns to the TV set. 'Damn. The news is over. See . . . because of you

I missed the cricket score and headlines.' The woman points out that the same bulletin will be repeated an hour later. He grumbles, 'It's not the same thing. I tell you, a man comes home dead beat . . . for what? To relax a little. What does he get? Tension. One of these days I'll get a heart attack and die. Because of you.'

The woman slinks out of the room miserably, feeling completely crushed. The man switches channels. His frown is deeper. His mouth twisted. The woman knows. She has erred. Again. There will be hell to pay. But before that, he needs his physical release. He's had a tough day at work. Period or no period, she'll have to oblige. Especially tonight. The children are waiting for her outside the bedroom door. 'Is daddy in a bad mood?' they ask. 'No. He's just tired. Daddy needs some peace. Leave him alone.' The kids exchange looks and say, 'Okay. Daddy's work is important. Now how about dinner? We're famished.'

Men At Home

Men like their homes till the age of seven. After that home becomes pure hell and they can't wait to get away. Even seemingly passive little boys dream about the day they can pack their little bags and push off as far away from the place they've been raised in as possible. Why? Sociologists will tell you it's the old hunting instinct. I say it's bad food. Most men hate what they eat in their own homes, even if they have gourmet chefs producing fancy eight-course meals twice a day or a wife who slaves over the kitchen fires preparing her man's favourite daal. If it's the wife who's doing the cooking, she is a loser even before she has begun because, as everybody knows by now, no wife can cook like the man's mother. So why bother trying? If it's a competent cook that's on the job, he is likely to have an ugly nose, unruly hair and a surly manner—and that, of course, affects the essential taste of the food. Even if cooksie is a gorgeous, twenty-one-year old wench, the fact that she is in the kitchen upto her arms in flour, takes away from her sex appeal. The same person in the neighbour's flat instantly becomes an object of desire and beauty whose pakoras deserve the highest culinary prize in the land. There is an unwritten adage in men's minds and it says, 'There's no food like home food.' The insult is cleverly built into this deceptive-sounding phrase.

Most men dislike their home environment as well. They complain constantly about dust nobody else sees, or yucky smells nobody else discerns. Their pillows and mattresses are never right. And the sight of a child's soft toy on the television set can drive them crazy. This is when they have families of their own.

Teenagers hate home on a very basic, personal level. They hate home because they have no other choice but to live there. This makes them feel trapped and resentful even if the mother does lose on an average five kilos a week picking up after them and making sure they are adequately fed sixteen times a day. The other guy's home is always better. Bigger. Cleaner. Noisier. Even the roach-infested hostel room some of the other guys occupy is preferable to their 'pads'—and who cares about the air-conditioning, private phone line, room service, laundered sheets, fresh underwear, freshly ironed clothes, clean sneakers and matched socks. Hey, this is no big deal, they say to their harried mothers. All the guys they know get this and more, like mushroom quiche for breakfast. And enough pocket-money to underwrite all those rising expenses.

Young men hate home because they feel they have to. And they believe they have no real business living in a place that isn't really 'theirs'. But the minute they do get 'their' own place, they start hating that too. It has nothing to do with the actual apartment/villa/penthouse/barsaati. It has to do with responsibility. Men don't enjoy running a home and dealing with boring stuff like veggies in the fridge, bills that need to be paid, dirty pots and pans in the sink, beds to be made—even if they do have servants to handle all that. It's the *thought*—that at the end of the day, the buck and the bakwaas ends with them—that causes the rebellion. They want to be little boys whose toys will be picked up and put away by someone, leaving them free to do the real stuff—like heavy-duty masturbation, for instance. They feel they have been forced (nasty society strikes again) to play adults with adult responsibilities. They claim they are indifferent to niceties and neat homes. That isn't true at all. What they mean is, they want someone else to deal with the mess—preferably a loving, even-tempered, efficient sex goddess who'll make their bed and lie on it later. Fine. The sex goddess won't mind rendering domestic and sexual services provided there's something in it for her—like appreciation and a couple of deluxe annual holidays.

Men like to see themselves as adventurers and nomads. Explorers of new worlds. Swashbuckling heroes. Daring lovers. They don't need four, boring walls with peeling paint to hem them in and kill their spirit. They want to roam the earth looking for . . . for . . . themselves, I guess. Unfortunately, when they do find their true persons, they think generally in terms of digging a large hole and burying themselves in it. So what? The imagination knows no boundaries. They let it soar foolishly as they plan impossible conquests, dream of seducing Madonna or Madhuri Dixit, buying an island off the coast of Greece, inventing a system likely to alter the way humanity functions, give Bill Gates a run for his money—get fame, fortune and fucks galore—just by staying away from home. Wise women understand this need and do not protest too strongly when their mates push off on a Sunday morning to play golf or have a haircut. They know that while they sweat it out and cut if off, their men will actually be elsewhere—in Lapland or Lakshwadeep, fantasizing about a new world order over which they they hold absolute sway.

It's rather sweet, when you think of it. Try tapping into the unconscious of a pot-bellied, ugly bear of a man sitting next to you on a plane. Just under that dull, complacent surface will be a closet conquistador raring to go and slay . . . someone . . . anyone. A business rival, an out-of-reach woman. The man with his nose buried in a business paper will in all likelihood be thinking about his erection and what he's going to do with it (aah—an erection of such immense proportions deserves nothing less than to slip smoothly into that busty woman in a blue saree sitting two seats down the aisle). Home will certainly not be on his mind. He has left it far behind him. He is on an airplane, escaping from bhindi masala and a clogged toilet. Exotic adventures await him at his destination—even if it is Jabalpur. There will be women and food unlike anything he gets at home. Life will hold out promise once more. There will be a reason to live. To battle on. Because home is so far away . . . so remote. He doesn't need reminders.

Home represents tyranny (even if it's only a sweet, fat, little wife asking for milk money and a little something for Pappu's school project). Home restricts freedom. A man's chance to express himself. Home imprisons. Home is a cage. Home, finally, is the villain. It is what keeps him shackled, unable to walk away and discover the true meaning of life—which is being an unshaven, unwashed, foul-mouthed slob even on Sundays, besides never changing his underwear.

Women think on a different plane. Home is security. Permanency. Stability. Aspects of domesticity that are anathema to most men. Women dream about perfect homes with good plumbing and at least one solid steel almirah to store the gold in. Men dream about perfect affairs—uncomplicated, secret and exciting. Home means everything to a woman. It means very little to a man.

Women can spend hours planning changes— new curtains, a darling settee, potted plants in the balcony, granite slabs in the kitchen, a maroon potty in the guest bathroom, the silver *paandaan* from the antique dealer, carpets— even a bright red garbage pail to liven up the dull kitchen. Men are happy kicking open an overstuffed suitcase and sleeping soundly on an unmade bed. They don't see paint peeling off the wall or frayed dhurries at their feet. They aren't pretending—they have selective vision. They don't care if the toilets are never cleaned or if the stuffing has come out of the armchair. Home can be a filthy hole in the wall provided there is enough booze around and a couple of magazines to flip through near the toilet seat.

They cannot connect with a woman's preoccupations. What does it matter, they ask exasperatedly, if the fucking sofa has no springs in it? Who needs springs? What if the fridge looks like a rare and unrecognizable contraption from the last century—it cools, doesn't it? And why all the fuss over a dining table that has lost a leg? Plates don't actually slide off it, do they? Women who go on about bedspreads and sideboards bug most men intensely with their whingeing. The surest way to cool down an amorous chap when he gets 'that' look in his eyes is to point out a coffee stain on a runner or mention the fact that the bedroom looks a mess because there is just no place to keep his law books since he refuses to buy a bookshelf. Phut! Down goes the little boodie-doodie as he pulls up his underpants and marches into the bathroom to gargle with his favourite mouthwash. To remind him of his petulance on his return is to ask for trouble. He has sex on his mind, woman, not shelves. And, as he's bound to throw it at you someday—your timing stinks.

When it comes to home repairs, however, there is no such thing as good timing. If you are foolish enough to wait for it, you will wait in vain—it might be fourteen long years before he notices the state of the ragged upholstery or the tattered cushion covers. The choice is yours— sex or a new washing machine? For most women the answer is obvious. How can sex possibly compete with a spin dryer?

Today's woman does not wait for her man to

sanction anything—not even their divorce proceedings. She goes ahead and buys what she thinks the home requires using that amazing modern convenience known as a credit card. She expects him to notice small changes around the house, but if he doesn't see the four-door refrigerator even while removing ice cubes from it, or wonder why he is sleeping on a twin bed after years spent by your side in a king-sized one, that's his problem. She has done what any sensible gal would do in her place—redecorate. And rearrange the furniture. If he miscontrues this act of friendship and commitment as a hostile one, too bad.

All changes around the house are seen by a man as part of a bigger conspiracy. Don't bother to reassure him or even set the record straight. A woman is entitled to a few perks—like a steam-iron that takes the wrinkles out of his pants or a new basin for him to spit in. Don't feel defensive and apologetic about home appliances either. Tell him you sincerely felt there was a serious vacuum in your life which could only be filled by the laser disc and C.D. player. Make him squirm with guilt for having the gall to question you. Demonstrate the power of the machines in the quality of your lives. Convince him that such domestic improvements can only be good for sex—that should clinch matters. Anything that's good for sex is good, period. However, be warned that this argument

134 O *The Portable Man*

does have its limits. You cannot, realistically speaking, talk him into believing that a psychedelically painted ceiling fan will in fact give you bigger, better 'O's.

But who says you can't try?

en On Holiday

Holidays make men horny. There is no logic behind this phenomenon. Just accept it for what it is—a fucking fact of vacation-life. And thank your stars you and not some busty bimbo in a drenched saree are around to be at the receiving end of his lust That is, if his horniness is a troublesome issue in the first place. If you welcome it, or conversely, if you plan your holidays using it as a promise—you can lie back and enjoy the ride. But if you are the kind who thinks in terms of hiking, swimming, sight-seeing or shopping, prepare youself for the inevitable. It is most likely that your best-laid plans to go wander through some tropical rain forest, chasing enormous butterflies, will be shot down just as you're getting your boots on. You will hear a voice from under crumpled sheets calling out, 'Hey Sexy—where do you think you're going?'

Don't ignore it. Don't go on lacing your boots. Kick them off and climb right back into bed . . . and remind yourself you'll be saving time and energy eventually. To resist at this point is to risk a fight. A good girl will meekly take off her clothes and submit. The hike can wait—or else, you'll be asked to take a permanent one yourself.

Men behave like spoilt kids when on vacation. They behave like that even when they aren't holidaying but it's easier to bear then since they aren't in your hair but driving someone else crazy in the office. Many couples confront their basic incompatibility while morosely staring at a vivid sunset at some exotic destination. The man may actually be eyeing a sexy, bikini-clad babe on a foreign beach and wondering to himself what the hell he's doing with the frumpy woman in an ugly salwar-suit sitting by his side greedily counting dollars. She may be experiencing similar doubts while remembering an old beau or the next-door-neighbour's son.

A recent television commercial advertising a smart new TV set caught the mood perfectly when it showed a buck-toothed businessman glibly lying on the phone to his unattractive wife, while a resort-bimbo fed him grapes.

Holidays make people get out of their city

skins and take a good, hard look at themselves. Men, of course, see a totally different image as they survey themselves in the hotel mirror. While the wife casts her critical eye over a bandy-legged buffoon in gaudy bermudas, he sees a dashing hero with the ability to slay a woman with his looks at fifteen paces. Wives don't feel threatened. They feel amused. And occasionally embarrassed, especially if the man decides to make a complete ass of himself in a post-dinner limbo competition. But women being more indulgent in these matters, they generally pretend they haven't noticed the sniggers and make the man feel less foolish about himself as he staggers back to the table, a moronic smile splitting his face.

Men aren't half as tolerant—heaven help a wife who dares to cross the line and kick up her heels in the arms of a dishy stranger. There is no forgiveness or understanding as the man glowers dangerously in the wings waiting for her to finish her little jig and get back to her senses. Then she has to prepare herself for a different dance step altogether since it's likely to be to his tune.

Prolonged and enforced togetherness such as a long trip necessarily implies, can be disastrous for a marriage. Couples who embark on month-long vacations do so at great peril to their relationship. I include honeymoons in this category. Adult people require private time and private spaces. Men rarely give women time off to just be by themselves. This lack of consideration gets exaggerated on foreign soil where men tend to behave like infants who have still to be toilet-trained. If a woman is accustomed to being on call constantly, she may be better able to cope with a man on holiday who refuses to get out of bed and draw the blinds or pick up the phone for room service.

Men expect their wives to turn into maids-cum-mistresses the moment they walk into a hotel room. They can never locate the keys to the suitcases, for example, and blame the spouse for forgetting to pack rubber chappals. They can't find small change either or notes of a modest denomination. This can be awfully annoying when a bellboy is standing around hopefully for a tip.

Men also suffer from a strange compulsion to remove all their clothes the moment they reach a new destination. While this is maybe a part of their holiday horniness, it's bloody inconvenient for a woman. It is she, the fully dressed one, who has to answer the door, pick up calls, fetch glasses of water, deal with porters and generally take charge. And all this while she's still wearing the tall stiletto heels which pinch her. Why? Because there is a stark naked man hiding under the covers with a silly grin on his face. Why is this man naked? Because he has read somewhere that men should strip and do a skin-to-skin the minute they get to their holiday destinations. And why should they be in such a hurry to strip? Because every minute counts. There is no time to lose. The meter is ticking. The jumbo erection, which is making the bed-clothes resemble a tent, might go down. The first appointment is an hour away. The shower cabin in the bathroom holds out an erotic promise. The wife's ass looks good from this angle. And what the hell, that's what men—real men—are supposed to do on holiday. Screw their brains out.

Women, on the other hand, look forward to relaxing on vacations. They have rest on their mind, not sex. Even honeymooners. One of the most civilized honeymoons I got to hear about involved a party of thirty friends of the newlyweds. After a seven-year-long courtship, the couple decided it would be much more fun to convert their seven days at a resort into a non-stop party. They were right. Their college mates looked at it as a reunion, they themselves behaved graciously as good hosts should and everybody had a great time. Most honeymoons turn out to be anything but sweet because the bride and groom want entirely different things out of the experience. The groom feels obliged to pounce on her at all times and anywhere just because that's what (he imagines) honeymooners round the world and down the centuries have always done. And she spends most of her waking hours wondering how to distract the fellow, get him off her aching back, rest her numb limbs a little, take care of the soreness spreading through most of her orifices . . . and maybe eat a little? Get up and pee? Wash her hair? Watch TV?? Talk to her mother? Check the weather outside their love nest? Shave her legs in privacy? Does she get to do any of that? Absolutely not, she is the man's sex-slave for the duration of the holiday and if she wants to get through the break without a breakdown of her marriage/ relationship, she'd do well to play along and pretend she can't get enough of it.

Men forget to eat on these love-fests . . . but they certainly don't forget to drink. Between bouts in bed, they muster up enough energy to stagger towards something tall, cold and alcohol-based. Fortified and energized, they jump right back into bed once their blood gets hot enough to reach all the right spots. The booze break is all a woman is likely to get to catch her breath and brush her teeth, so it's best she rushes to the loo while the guy knocks back his beer and stays there till she hears a low, throaty growl summoning her back to where she belongs—in bed. Exhaustion and a little boredom start to set in approximately five days down the line—but don't bet on it. If your partner is a marathon man out to break records, he'll make sure you keep up. Some sweeten the experience/ordeal with honey-soaked words, others show their appreciation in more tangible ways—gifts and promises of better things to follow. Foolish women fall for the oldest con word in the world, 'Later', and lie back against crumpled sheets, eyes shut, teeth clenched, legs parted. There is no 'later', of course. But, as the experienced will ask tiredly— what is the option anyway?

Separate vacations, for one. But not too many men agree to such an arrangement. Primarily because most lack the drive, energy and confidence to go in search of sex partners on solo trips. Wives and girlfriends are far more convenient. There is very little a sexed-out woman can do when she's stuck at a remote resort, her passport and ticket in the safe custody of the partner. She can eat onions and garlic. Refuse to shave her armpits. Stop using a deodorant. And definitely do without musky perfume. But, does the man notice or care? Hell no—he's on holiday. And he's horny.

Besides, he's picking up all the tabs. Which means he can have sex on demand. And you are on call day or night. It's all right, honey. It could be worse. You could be dancing naked by the pool without him noticing. Now, that would not be good for any self-respecting gal's morale. To say nothing of her reputation.

Cheer up. You don't have to do this sort of thing everyday. Only twice a year. The rest of the time he has his pillow. And his income tax returns. And you have *TNT*.

The Inner Man

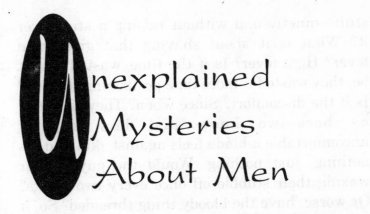

Unexplained Mysteries About Men

Take it from me, these are best left unexplained. Though it does make us girls wonder sometimes. Here are examples worth pondering (but not worth losing any sleep) over.

Mystery Number One: Why do guys hate shaving?

Think about it. Have you ever met a man who looked at his razor/shaver with anything less than pure hatred? Have you met a man who has taken this innocuous daily ritual in his stride and just done it—like he does other daily stuff—quietly and without raising a stink over it? What is it about shaving that gives men fever? High fever? Is it the time 'wasted'—can't be, they waste far more time postponing shaving? Is it the discomfort? Since when? They can't fool us here—we know just how slightly uncomfortable a blade feels against skin and it's nothing, just nothing. Would the guys prefer waxing their stubble off once every two weeks? Or worse, have the bloody thing threaded? So, it isn't the pain and it isn't the time. What is it?

They brush their teeth without too much of a fuss—well, most of them do. All right, they cheat when it comes to regular flossing. But come shaving-hour and the grumbling begins.

And yet, young boys with whiskers can't wait to get their hands on daddy's (or mummy's) razor. At age twelve or thirteen, shaving is one of two most desirable activities (you can guess the other one). Once they start getting the fuzz off on a daily basis they're ready for the serious grown-up stuff. Shaving is their badge, part of the 'official adult' kit—and they can't get enough of it (or the other activity). In fact, some of them love it so much they rush around looking for shaving foam at odd hours, practically minutes after their last session. That's because young boys don't miss a single chance to gaze at themselves in the mirror. They love their own image. They love the sight of a face covered with lather. It makes them feel forty years old. Oh-

oh—maybe we've hit it there. When these same chaps actually hit forty, that's when they can't stand to look at themselves first thing in the morning.

Understandable—yes, girls? We've been there. We know the feeling. But that's only part of the resentment. Men seem to detest shaving with a vengeance. Which is why they go into instant bum-mode over weekends. Notice their unshaven chins, those dreadful, crumpled lungis, hung-over puffy eyes and lank hair in dire need of a shampoo? Yuck! Is this the man you gave it all up for? Do you really want to cohabit with a slob? Think about it, guys. It's almost as bad as a woman who defiantly hangs around in a haldi-stained housecoat with unshaven legs and mascara smudged down to her chin, 'because it's Sunday'.

Mystery Number Two: Ever met a man who doesn't hide newspapers and magazines till he's absolutely and totally through with them? No? Neither have I. Men are pathological in this area. I don't know what it is that makes them go to impossible lengths sometimes just in order to deprive the rest of the family from getting their hands on the dailies. Is it because they don't wish to share info? Is it a conspiracy to keep everybody around them dumb and ignorant so that they themselves shine? Do they do something secret with these papers that we women can never guess at? Are they just slow readers? Do they hate the thought of someone else getting to know something before they do? Is it because they usually pay the paper bills and therefore feel possessive about the paper? Who knows? Young men, middle-aged men, old men . . . watch them swoop on the dailies with a manic gleam in their eyes and you'll wonder what it is that they feel so triumphant about. Ask them politely to give you one of those three newspapers they're clutching close to their chests and they'll growl, 'Later,' before marching off to the best reading chair in the home. Go further and ask for at least one section of the paper (the one that features movie stars and models) and they'll look at you like you're crazy, 'What? Give you four whole sheets? Why?' 'Because you have thirty unread ones still in your hand,' you might bleat pathetically. Will that make the man relent and hand over your favourite sections in a friendly-like manner? Not a chance. More likely, he'll place the other papers under him—literally sit on them—till he's good and ready to declare he's through. And then he'll behave like he's being extraordinarily magnanimous as he walks over to where you're sulking—newspapers held out in the place of a white flag.

It doesn't end there. Men *love* hiding stuff—and this includes magazines and books. I'm not talking about only the girlie rags carrying pictures of naked bimbos with pneumatic breasts. Just regular journals everybody likes to flip

through. You'll be lucky if you get old issues—
but even those will have to be ferreted out from
assorted corners where they've been stashed
away to be read another day. Latest issues
disappear into a black hole the moment they're
delivered. Often the man forgets where he has
buried them and accuses the woman of the
house of (a) theft or (b) illegal concealment. No
amount of explanations/protestations/temper
tantrums can convince the fellow to the contrary.
He smells a conspiracy . . . and storms out of the
house and to the nearest bar. A woman who
waits her turn to get a look-see at the headlines
is a woman who knows her place in the general
scheme of things (at the bottom of the pile,
hon—where else did you think?)

Mystery Number Three: Men need to be potty-
trained and house-broken if you are to live
happily ever after with them. Like frisky puppies
with full bladders and nervous guts, guys too
have to be gently taught how to . . . ummm . . .
use the facilities. Most of them genuinely don't
know; they *think* they do, but their mothers
haven't taught them better. Also, their mothers
have mopped up after them efficiently and
silently for so long, they've never had to look
back or clean their own messes. Just like puppies
and crawling infants. However, unlike puppies,
men don't respond too well to paper training.
You know what I mean: tap the doggy on the
nose with a tightly rolled-up newspaper, shove

his face into the poop and say 'Naughty, naughty' in your sternest voice—the pooch gets the messge by and by. This method is not recommended for men who share your space—though it's hard not to want to give it a go. There are other 'reward-and-punishment' routes—you have to keep working on yours till the guy gets it right. It's important not to feel too discouraged if he continues to make mistakes during the first few months of training. Avoid spanking, kicking, cursing or any other form of corporal punishment. Try inducements instead. Sexual favours for exceptional bladder-and-bowel control might sound unfair—but hey—how important are clean, neat loos to you? Very? Then don't argue.

Once the man realizes (c'mon—give him his due, even dumb puppies get the message soon enough) that leaving dirty clothes on the bathroom floor or kicking discarded undies over closets doesn't exactly endear him to his beloved, he'll stop. The next stage to aim for is basic basin etiquette. It's not a particularly friendly gesture for a man to mess up the place with dental floss, shaving cream, toothpaste foam, various effluvia, falling hair and clipped nose/ear hairs. Puddles of water aren't very chummy either. Women hate wet bathroom floors (I guess men hate them too, even when they've done all the wetting). And they like their men to aim straight while peeing. I'm not even getting into the worldwide debate over seat-up, seat-down.

Compared to the revulsion provoked by the sight of pee all over the toilet seat, that's nothing.

Are women being a bit too finicky? Irritatingly fastidious? Not at all. So many marriages would be saved if only men behaved like civilized considerate creatures. Try turning the tables— do women leave their feminine thingies lying around? Does a man like to use the loo that has just been vacated by a woman who has left evidence of her lunar cycle all over the place? Do men enjoy the sight of bras and panties lying carelessly everywhere? Do they really want to use face towels stained with lipstick, mascara, foundation, rouge—something even worse? Does the sight of long strands of hair clogging the drains turn anybody on? Is leaving toilet bags full of make-up near his shaving mirror such a great idea? We all agree these strictly constitute a no-no. Well then, what is the solution? Simple— separate bathrooms. (Some would extend that to separate bedrooms as well, but that's taking it a bit too far—unless you are seventy-plus and employ a night nurse who fetches you bed-pans every half-hour.

Living with a man requires reserves that cannot be quantified. If your chap never ever remembers to replace the toothpaste top, dry the platform surrounding the basin, put back his shaving things, screw back the cap on the after-shave . . . and yes . . . often forgets to flush— seriously—divorce is the only way out.

Mystery Number Four: Notice how some guys turn into boors the minute they walk into a restaurant? (And these guys aren't boors to begin with.) Put them in any other situation and chances are they'll behave themselves. Walk them past the etched glass door of a tony eatery and something snaps. You know the syndrome: first, the chap assumes a disdainful expression as he glares around him. Then his eyes lock with the maitre d's. If a fistfight doesn't follow immediately, count till twenty, it will. Later, he might explain it wasn't anything personal, but tailcoats invariably did that to him. If the maitre d' survives, the waiter won't. By then your escort is itching to punch the fellow in the nose. Before the evening is over, you bet he will. A wise woman recognizes the signs when she sees them (flared nostrils, heavy breathing, arm-hairs bristling). At this point she can do three things: (a) join another table and break up a marriage (b) play footsie with her guy (c) feign a bellyache and insist on leaving. Whichever way she *plays* it, the man will be furious. He is there to fight with everybody, see? You are cheating him out of a bloody free-for-all.

Men with chips on their shoulders get an instant complex when they spot good-looking waiters—especially if the good-looking waiters gel their hair. Gelled hair, good looks and tails, as any female who has ever loved Clark Gable will assure you, have the effect of turning her knees into jelly. Alas, some women are born restaurant coquettes. Their eyelashes begin to flutter during the car ride itself. But they only go into brazenly flirtatious mode once they have a menu card in their hands. If a man wishes to avoid a scene he should make sure his date never gets to glance through one. Be masterful and in control, guys. Say in a voice that does not tolerate another's opinion, 'Filet mignon for her and several double whiskies on the rocks for me—yes—as apertifs, starters, main course and dessert.' If that doesn't work and she continues to make goo-goo eyes at Marc (why are good-looking, gelled-haired waiters the world over all called 'Marc'?)—there's trouble ahead. Some men deal with it by creating a scene and sending back the food. Others make utter fools of themselves being superior about the wine. Still others crib about the slow service, the uncomfortable seating arrangements, the piped music . . . even the candlelight ('Why can't you people invest in decent candles that don't drip into souffles?') Right.

Women squirm through these evenings (when they aren't flirting with the waiter) and end up going to bed awfully hungry. The couple drive back in silence. She sulks for months. He goes home and drinks some more. She dreams she is naked and dancing the tango with the waiter, next to a softly-lit swimming pool. He blames her for ruining the evening. She reminds him it wasn't her who started it all by mispronouncing 'Bordeaux' and getting furious with the waiter for saying 'Sir?' in that awful way waiters have of putting creeps in their proper places. He stares at the astronomical bill he has brought away with him and snaps, 'What a waste, I could get a crate of whisky for the same price.' She says, 'Absolutely. And I could stay home and eat daal chaval in peace.' The children wake up and ask, 'Are you two fighting again?' And the man says, 'Of course not. What made you think that?' The woman rolls her eyes meaningfully.

The bottom line is this: men detest fancy restaurants where they have to sit around stiffly and pretend to enjoy food they cannot identify, from a menu card they can't read, and served by a good-looking waiter with gelled hair whom their wives have spent the entire evening making meaningful eye contact with. No. This isn't their idea of a great outing. Plus, what they resent the most is that they have to pay for the effing thing at the end of it. Take-away pizzas are a far better idea on days you are feeling lazy/romantic; your guy doesn't have to meet the delivery boy. You do. Make sure you have lashings of mascara on when that doorbell rings. You never know. He could be good-looking with gelled hair—and be named Marc.

Mystery Number Five: 'Let that thing alone.' The minute you hear a guy utter those words, just move over calmly and allow him to electrocute himself/blow his brains out/saw off his leg/start a fire. Never ever try to separate a man from his gizmos. There is an invisible circuitry at work here that you cannot even begin to fathom.

Machines are a major turn-on for guys. Women are sensible about anything that requires to be plugged into a socket (sex included). They learn to leave life-threatening, wired stuff alone. But not men. Show them a machine and they'll want to take it apart instantly. Inside every man is a mechanic who swears he knows how everything in the world works. Everything, including a nuclear reactor. Give him the chance and he's ready to attack with nothing more complicated than a screwdriver to assist him. The more menacing-looking the machine, the greater his adrenalin rush. The reason men make absolute fools of themselves over inanimate objects that can't shout back or withhold sexual favours, is because those things make them feel powerful and useful.

Formula One drivers are about the cockiest fellows around. Why? It is the ultimate ride—driving machines put together with millions of dollars of the sponsors' money, tearing down a racing track at unbelievable speed while bimbos in the pit stop wet their panties with each heart-stopping lap. And it's those guys crouched behind what look like toy wheels who control all

the action; create speed records; spray the
adoring crowds with champagne. They are
literally and figuratively in the driver's seat. Oh
man, this is macho-heaven. Life in the fast
track can't get faster.

If your chap wants to give Schumacher a run
for his money as he zooms down Marine Drive
in his beat-up Maruti—let him. Do not discuss
boring stuff like speed-breakers and red lights.
The guy and his machine are bonding. It is a
sublimely male moment. Of course, *you* are
going to end up climbing the next lamp-post.
And *you'll* be the one arranging for a tow-car.
So, what? He has had his big moment with his
machine. And there's always WIAA for you.

Mystery Number Six: Strange how mild-
mannered mousikins break into a rash when
they see a woman on a telephone. It affects
them deeply. Their voices change, eyeballs bulge
and their body lingo alters in a manner so
menacing, family dogs run for cover. Family
dogs. Not the woman on the phone. You see she
can't quite *see* at that point. She's on the phone.
Bell's invention has that effect on women. It
renders them instantly blind. Not only can they
not see stuff that's right under their noses, they
can't smell either. A dish could burn to cinders
on the gas range. Smoke might billow out from
the kitchen and sting everybody else's eyes.
There could be a short-circuit somewhere. An
earthquake under their feet. A man could fly

past the window. The servants could be copulating on the living room floor. Does the woman-on-the-phone notice?

Naah. She is on the phone . . . *it is the single most important act in her busy day*. Her friend has just finished telling her that the tycoon in the penthouse next door is having it off with that bitch with the great butt—yes, yes, the same one who comes to the health club in leopard-print leotards. Not her! Yes, her. But wasn't she having a little thingie with her husband's best friend . . . or one of the butlers from 'The Zodiac Grill'? No, no, no—the masseur at the fitness centre. That's right. Mr Cutie with the oily curls. This is unbelievable. What's wrong with these people? And to think the tycoon's daughter is getting married in summer. Imagine. Of course the wife has taken it badly. She has stopped wearing pink. It's only black these days. Yeah, her form of protest. Not that it suits her. I mean how many forty-somethings have you seen who can wear black at a club luncheon and not look like out-of-work witches. No, that's not being bitchy, never. Just honest.

It is at this precise moment that guys explode. The outburst takes many forms. Either an angry voice bellows, 'Hey, get off that bloody line—I'm expecting a call. An important call.' The woman doesn't react because the woman hasn't heard. Really, she isn't pretending. She isn't being difficult. She genuinely hasn't heard a word.

Her ears are still burning with 'the news' (Pinkie has eloped with her best friend's driver, and the best friend is furious—she can't drive. She's stuck—over a menial's fuck).

The man stops bellowing and strides up to the woman. She still doesn't see him. He grabs the receiver from her hot little hands. She continues talking (by now she's on auto pilot, see?). He barks into the instrument and bangs it down firmly. Aah—now he's talking. *Bam!* The woman wakes up. She snaps out of her trance and glares at the cockroach who has dared to cut her off. The cockroach behaves like cockroaches generally do—he crawls away from the source of heat and light into a safe, dark corner and stays there. That is, if he's wise. Only a foolish man starts an argument at this stage and demands explanations. 'What if someone were trying to get through? My mother could by dying. There could be an emergency. I was expecting an important call.'

'So how come men are always expecting 'important calls' which never materialize? How come they invariably find just that one minute/ two hours/longer to make or take that call, *just* when women are about to crack something impossibly mystical over the wire? Why can't men understand that women and phones are linked not merely by a long plastic cord but an umbilical one? Phones are their lifeline to the outside world. It's a primal need for them to communicate with someone who's actually listening . . . and not pretending to listen. The phone equals friendship, acceptance, information . . . love. It keeps loneliness away. It connects them to themselves more than to whosoever is on the other side. Phones are their all-purpose therapeutic answers. They're better than sedatives, cigarettes or booze. Many a marriage has been salvaged thanks to an unpretentious little instrument that goes trring-ring, trring-ring.

A sensible man ought to co-opt these little guys. It's better to have them on the right side than risk blood clots, strokes, cardiac arrest, hernia—particularly hernia. Men just have to come to terms with the talking-machine. Look at it this way, guys—it's far better to keep the little woman yackity-yakking away with another little woman than have her running around chasing other gals' husbands with more moolah and raging testosterone-levels or seducing alarmingly young door-to-door salesmen peddling vacuum cleaners along with their gym-toned bods. It's a toss-up then, between a telephone and a toy-boy. Take your pick.

Men And Their Mothers

J have never understood why wives and girlfriends get so worked up over other women when the only woman worth taking serious note of in their partner's life is the mother. I have also never understood why this lady makes everybody so nervous. Sensible spouses should not even attempt to compete with their men's mamas. It's a total waste of time and counter-productive too. Befriending the enemy isn't always the answer, but as strategies go, it beats battling with the old bird.

Men love their mothers. Men only love their mothers. Men love their mothers only. That covers most of the ground, I should think.

It's true. The mama-bond is a very special one. Once you accept its existence and decide not to challenge it, you are better off. How can you possibly compete with a creature who has been certified perfect by the man you love? Perfect is perfect, right? If you have problems with that, too bloody bad. Not all men are upfront about the way they feel towards their mommies. Some hide their feelings better than others, some feel apologetic about revealing the depth of their emotion and some make excuses for the way they feel even when nobody has asked. It's all right. Men are like that when it comes to things that they're sentimental about. Like belts with broken buckles. Or toothbrushes that resemble toilet cleaners. They get defensive and possessive faced with a choice. Don't force him to make one. Don't say things like 'It's either her or me. Those awful old things or my love.' They're pretty sure in their minds and you end up looking a fool when the decision is taken. It's always 'her' and 'those things' over you. Get it?

Wives should leave men alone to handle their mothers. But they don't. They like to think their husbands want their participation in pampering their mummies. They don't. It's a private affair between a grown man and the woman from whose womb he has entered the world. It's biological bonding that excludes you.

Who are you to him, anyway? A prettyish stranger he cast lustful eyes on years and years ago? What is your real *rishta* with the guy? Wouldn't the logical question to ask be, '*Hum Aapke Hain Kaun?*' Nothing. Is there a blood link? No. An umbilical cord? No. Will he die without you? Absolutely not. Will he die without his mother? Yes. Is she replaceable? No way. And you? Any day. Even if you have borne the man children he claims he loves dearly? Yes. Do you hate him for this? No. You hate his mother.

Well—don't. It isn't her fault she has a milksop for a son. She can't help it if he still makes goo-goo eyes at her or starts sucking his thumb in her awesome presence. Has she asked him to sit at her feet and press them? Is it the mother who insists on spoonfeeding this hulk you're married to each time you visit her home? Isn't it the hulk who regresses to the extent of adopting a baby-voice and going in for childish prattle whenever she's in the vicinity? Okay, she does treat him like he's a naughty five-year-old—but she's his mother. To whom his childhood meant their best years together—do you mind? She can still remember how he used to snuggle up to her and fall fast asleep while she lovingly cleaned his nostrils/ears. Or how sweetly he presented his bottom to be washed after doing a big poo-poo at the dining table. These are indelible memories. You only came into the picture after the hulk was toilet-trained. You didn't get the golden chance to wipe his bum. You refuse to take the lint out of his belly-button. You even refuse to trim his ear/nostril hairs. And you dare to talk about love and devotion?

Don't fool yourself, woman. True love involves—yup—sacrifice and a willingness to get your hands dirty. You fail miserably in that department. Yes you do. Remember how you reacted to his snot-filled hankies—the undisguised disgust on your face? Or the rude way in which you held your nose when he removed his shoes and waved smelly socks in your face? His mother would never do that. Never. Nor would she refuse to wake up from deep sleep and fix him an omelette at two in the morning after he's come lurching back from a drinking binge with the 'boys'. Mothers love to wait up for their sons.

And you? Not only do you fall asleep, you do something far worse—you keep the television on. And the bathroom light too. And that's not all. You deliberately forget to keep his pajamas neatly folded on the bed. Plus, the covers aren't turned down on his side. A man walks in wearily and somewhat blearily into his bedroom after a long, long day, seeking comfort and iced water. He's willing to settle for a Bloody Mary and an omelette. What does he find? A woman in a crumpled nightie fast asleep with the lights and television on. Is that fair? Should she not be sitting by the door with the cocktail in her hand and a smile on her face? What do you mean that's·unreasonable? Nothing is unreasonable— that's the least a breadwinner expects. Food and basic amenities. He's paying for them, dammit.

Now take the man's mother. Would she squint back at him and ask a stupid question like, 'What time is it?' knowing full well she'll receive a wonky answer? Would she throw dirty looks in the drunk's direction and go right back to sleep? Would she yell, 'Stop making so much noise in the loo—you'll wake up the neighbourhood', thereby adding to the din? Would she refuse, yes, refuse, to go to the kitchen and heat up dinner for the fifth time in one night, saying, 'Nobody eats tandoori chicken at three in the morning in this house'? Never. Mothers understand perfectly that men have to be men. They cannot be stopped from or reprimanded for enjoying themselves from time to time.

You may not think much of men who knock back half-a-dozen whiskies on an empty stomach. It may not be *your* idea of enjoyment. So what? Who's asking you in the first place? Huh?? Who?? Does his mother ever so much as mention booze in his presence? Utter that awful word called 'alcohol'? Does her expression alter even one teensie-weensie bit when her son rolls in reeling? Of course not. She smiles indulgently, shoos all the servants away, scowls in your general direction and asks brightly, 'Hungry?

No problem. I'll quickly make some aloo parathas for you. Won't take a minute. Don't worry.'

Someday you'll be saying exactly the same thing to your bounder of a son. It's not just part of our mental make-up to behave thus as mothers, it's the movies that insist we do. Whether it was Nirupama Roy in the old days or Raakhee at present, all screen mums die for the opportunity of making aloo parathas for the drunken louts they call sons. Movie mothers hear no evil, see no evil and speak no evil when it comes to male offspring. These unworthy men may be murderers and/or rapists—but mama knows best. They've turned that way because of society—sorry—*society*. But because they've grown into great big hulking heroes on energy-giving, pure, unadulterated mother's milk, there beats a heart of gold under that hairy chest.

Now . . . if you're the materialistic kind who is after gold but not the heart, mama-dear will know soon enough. And then, she'll pass it on to sonny-boy. Remember—men and their mothers have no secrets between them. She knows every single aspect of your life together. *Every*. You think she doesn't know your menstrual cycle or that the two of you prefer the straight, old-fashioned missionary position? Ha! Do you really believe she is unaware of your predelictions and kinks? Wrong again. She probably even knows that you like waxing over shaving and that you don't floss on a regular basis. Why do you think the two of them exchange meaningful looks so frequently? What about all those *sotto-voce* phone calls between the two of them while you're showering? Or those cryptic, coded messages at the dinner table that nobody else is supposed to intercept or understand? You think he's ever going to tell you what *he* discusses with his mother? Forget it. Try confronting him and he'll deny it all. Lie through his teeth. Plus, call her up to report that you'd 'accused' him of conspiring against you with his own, sweet, gentle mother.

Some wives prefer denial. They like pretending they don't have a mother-in-law even when the old biddy is sitting right across them, stuffing her face with murgh masallam and glaring evilly. Women learn how to blank out unpleasant sights. And odours. Mothers-in-law exude a particular smell that is quite, quite distinctive to their breed. It doesn't matter where they come from, all of them send out the same scent. I believe it can be successfully bottled under an appropriate brand name, such as 'Hostility' or 'Suspicion'. Do sons smell what the world smells? Naturally not. They fill their nostrils with the world's headiest fragrance each time Mummyji walks into the room. 'Ecstasy?' 'Bliss?' 'Embrace?' All three. They call their wives 'paranoid' and insist they suffer from a persecution complex even when there is a full-fledged attack on their person in the man's presence. 'Calm down,' advises the *beta*. 'The way you're carrying on, one would think you were being nuked or something.' So you scream back, 'It's worse than nuking. At least there are bomb shelters around when wars break out. Where do I go?' Mummyji is likely to stop her verbal onslaught at this point and give you the mongoose-with-snake treatment. 'How about your father's house?' she might suggest maliciously, while the son cowers in the background . . . or worse, starts whistling tunelessly. At such times men favour the *Colonel Bogie March*, for some odd reason. Unintentionally perhaps, they're trying to tell their wives something. Like 'Start marching. Hup, two, three, four.'

Mothers-in-law prefer to take the sweet route out of a crisis. They waddle to the refrigerator, pick up a box of mithai, sit themselves comfortably in front of the video and start watching Madhuri Dixit, clad in a purple saree, bouncing her left hip while the soundtrack blasts, *'Mere Piya Ghar Aaya, O Ramji.'* The *piya* in question may genuinely be feeling penitent towards the wife by now, but will rarely show it. It's called the 'loyalty factor', and closely resembles the one that Delhi politicians frequently invoke when they're looking for berths in the Cabinet.

What is a smart, modern lady supposed to do when war breaks out? Howl and cry? Never. Apologize? Are you mad? Apologies can be held against a woman as irrefutable 'proof' of her guilt. You say 'sorry' and you're dead. Defiance? Depends. Generally speaking, Gandhiji's 'Satyagraha' strategy sucks. What I mean is, times have changed. Moral protests are no good. If you have to make a point, do so dramatically and at full blast. Embarrass the culprits—the shameless whistler and his mithai-gorging mother. Pump up the volume so that your voice can be heard from one end of the street to the other. If you do throw a fit, make it an absolute beaut. Rage, rave, rant, tear your hair out. Fling breakable stuff at the walls. Beat your breasts. Make sure the mascara doesn't run. Threaten to strip and expose your nakedness to the world. Nothing scares a man more than the thought that his wife's sacred body may be up for public viewing. It is the worst insult and deepest fear. After all, that body belongs exclusively to him and is for his eyes only. Never mind that the wife may be the beach bikini type of girl or even a former calendar pin-up. Once she's his, he has sole rights over her flesh—particularly when it's naked.

Men love their delusional worlds, so they'll want to cling to them. Start unbuttoning your shirt for starters. He'll stop whistling—that's for sure. He'll also leap at you and be there in one swift motion. Good. At least he's now on your side. Physically, at any rate. Now *she's* across enemy lines. Go for the kill. Keep unbuttoning—especially if there are servants around.

Remember that riveting scene in *Bandit Queen*, when Phoolan Devi is stripped and paraded naked in front of the villagers? Keep that on your mental screen. It is the ultimate degradation. After all, the film did win international recognition. So might you. Once the chap is next to you and grovelling pathetically, you can either throw them into a chill pool and leave him to freeze there, or cover him all over with sloppy, wet smackeroos. I mean *all over*. Especially if the old bird is watching (which of course she will be). Show her the power of sex, and watch her squirm. You might be tempted to giggle at this stage. Don't. If you have to make a statement, go all the way. Start unbuttoning *his* shirt this time. You can be reasonably sure that mother-in-law will cover her eyes, let out a scream and rush from the house, cursing you all the way. No problem. That's what you wanted—right?

You can stop the charade now. You don't really want the man who's staring awestruck at you while continuing to unbutton himself, do you? You do??? Okay, why not? It's called, 'making out and making up'. Turns some people on, too. Go for it. But puh*leeze*, not in the living room. Surely the domestics have seen enough for one day? Shift the action elsewhere. Like to the bathroom, for example. Do it under the shower. It's a pleasant way to cool off. Beats an air-conditioner or an orange squash.

Besides, mother-in-law will be on the phone shortly to check whether or not her son has obeyed her advice and flung you out—with clothes on, of course. The family's honour is at stake. It's one thing to throw out a fully-clad, crazy wife. Everybody understands that. The whole world knows it's her fault. Quite another to have the *bahu* of the *khandaan* be seen starkers as she sobs her way to her father's house. Now *that's* a scandal impossible to live down. When she does call, pin your man down (you'll know how) and tell him to tell her to 'F.O.'. Also tell him that you do not appreciate coitus interruptus. He may or may not pass this on to her—but you mean business. Don't let him leave the room for at least another hour. Insist on post-coital cuddling. Let her stew some more. If she happens to be stewing in the very next room, this is your chance to moan, groan, scream suggestively, growl and cry. If you don't know how, watch Sharon Stone in any film. Or Madonna's videos. You'll get the hang of it soon enough.

Sex has its uses—this is the time to exploit all of them. Make it an event, make sure your husband never forgets it. More than anything else, make sure your mother-in-law remembers each and every scintillating moment of the encounter—if she survives at all—and takes it to the grave with her.

Men's Fantasies

J know this is awfully hard to believe, but it has been reliably learnt that men have other things on their minds besides non-stop, heavy-duty sex. In fact they don't really think about sex all that much since they realize that thinking about it a lot is a clear indication that they aren't getting too much of it in reality. This is the sort of bad news men avoid—which is why they prefer to fantasize about money. Having scads of it. Even men with scads of money dream about having more of it. Money takes their minds off sex and makes them feel powerful.

All male fantasy is about power. About attaining godhood. Ask around. Ask that meek-looking clerk in the nationalized bank down the road. Go ahead. Ask him. He'll tell you what's on his mind and it will be money—not the bank's deposits, but his own personal lolly. Women find men's preoccupation with filthy lucre a little funny. They expect men to have better things on their minds—like them, for instance. Fat chance. The only time men actively try to translate their fantasies about women into reality is when their pockets are full—not surprisingly—since in their minds women and money are interlinked anyway.

How so? Simple. Men—even civilized, educated chaps (maybe them more than the poor *unpadhs* in bullock-carts), do think of females as commodities with a price-tag attached to **them**. Whether it's the marriage market or just a roll in the hay, they know there is money to be paid. The moment they fancy a woman they whip out their mental calculators to try and figure out the starting price and then work upwards. 'Will I be able to afford this broad?' they ask themselves worriedly, and then proceed to the actual sums.

If it's a short-term liaison they're looking at, it still involves a certain expense—maybe air tickets, five-star suite tariffs, champagne, flowers, gifts, phone bills and other minor frills which do not include serious jewellery. A long-term deal worries them still more since that translates into a major investment without assured returns. A glamorous friend told me about the time a prominent industrialist set up a fancy date with her. Twelve dozen (she counted) long-stemmed roses were delivered two hours before he was due to show up at her Parisian apartment. A case of champagne followed an hour later. Finally, the man himself appeared in a hired Bentley. They dined on caviar and suchlike at a fine Russian restaurant and drank some more champagne. Finally, he turned to her, grabbed her hand and asked significantly, 'What more do I have to do . . .?' The sentence was left deliberately incomplete. What he didn't say was this: 'What more do I have to do to get into your pants now that I have spent so much?' My girlfriend looked him straight in the eye and replied, 'What more? Nothing much. Just un-marry yourself.' He wasn't amused and he never saw her again.

Men like to see solid returns when they put their money down. That's when fantasy becomes a reality and they feel they're finally getting their money's worth. Money unfortunately always gets in the way—even when they're fantasizing about getting mouth-to-mouth resuscitation from Pamela Anderson. While they mentally swap places with the square-jawed Mitch, they start counting in dollars—can I really afford the *Baywatch* babe? If not, why don't I switch channels? While idly surfing they may come across an image that turns them on—an exposed leg, a bit of butt, a hint of cleavage. Of course, they want to sleep with whosoever is attached to whatever they've caught a glimpse of, but then they're jolted back into thinking about the price-tag and phut goes the fantasy.

Men are spectacularly unimaginative when it comes to articulating their secret ambitions. Ask them and they'll say they dream of switching places with the Sultan of Brunei. Why? Because he's the richest man on earth. They never reckon with a Bill Gates. Or even a Steven Spielberg. And what would they do in the Sultan's place? Why—screw their brains out with the world's most desirable women, naturally. That is, when they weren't making love to their billions.

Women lead rich, varied, adventurous fantasy lives. But that's also because reality sucks for most of them. The only way to survive and escape the dull, killing routine of their domestic prisons is to rely on imagination to transport them to higher planes. Places never seen, men never experienced, textures never felt, colours never created, fragrances never smelt. Women combine fantasies in the most ingenious ways—food and sex, for example, being the biggest turn-on. But unlike men, their sexual fantasies rarely go into overdrive at the sight or thought of a complete stranger. On the contrary, women's main fantasy, if the truth be told, is to escape men. Be free of their control, lead self-sufficient independent lives without obligation and duty. If that means permanent celibacy—so be it.

Abstinence is a very small price to pay for what they long for the most—freedom.

Men don't get it. They assume women crave for their bodies with the same sort of intensity with which men crave for women's. Not true. *Jonathan Livingstone Seagull* was definitely a 'she-gull' even if the author himself didn't know it.

Men's preoccupation with power is the other thing women find difficult to connect with. Nearly every aspect of a man's life is somehow linked with the acquisition and application of power. Just as men believe (rightly so) that money is power, they also think of their sexual prowess in power terms. When the two meet (money and sex), an aphrodisiac is born. Which is why short, fat, bald men with moolah often make it to the lists of the world's sexiest studs. Maybe they really are supermen in bed—but looking at them, who'd suspect? Countless gorgeous women, apparently, who'd then close their eyes and think of Richard Gere in *Pretty Woman*. The reason that film made millions is because it hooked into every woman's ultimate fairytale featuring a devastatingly handsome, loaded prince clad in a Cerruti suit installing them in a luxury suite and asking for nothing more than an off-camera b.j.

Some men have dirty fantasies involving innocent children. But we don't want to include perverts in our clean book, do we? Some men dream about making it with hookers. Sex on sale is a fairly common fantasy for guys who don't dare walk into the best little whorehouse in town but think incessantly about doing so.

Men also get it off on office colleagues—particularly subordinates. Sex with secretaries rates high on the fantasy scale—not surprisingly—it's one image that combines power with fornication, which adds up to perfect sex. I once asked an eighty-plus man if he still thought a lot about 'it'—and if he did was he frustrated because he couldn't really do anything in that department? He smiled and admitted he'd never once stopped thinking about sex . . . especially while channel-surfing. He'd look at a newsreader's low-necked blouse and imagine embracing her. He'd surreptitiously watch a neighbour's wife changing and try and visualize the shape of her breasts. He'd go to the market and lust after a vegetable-vendor. Did any of these fantasies disturb or bother him? Not at all. 'They add spice to my boring life,' he smiled. 'The day I stop thinking about women I'll know I am dead.'

It's a pity men's sexual fantasies remain at such a mundane, pedestrian level, rarely extending beyond 'doing it' with someone. Anyone. Even that ghastly woman walking down the street wearing a vomit-green saree. They can't help it if their imagination is that limited and they believe it's numbers that count. It has to do with their obsession with charts, figures, graphs and statistics. On an average day they congratulate themselves on ten mental copulations with anonymous women they know they'll never have in reality. But so what—ten is an impressive number.

And that's the romantic part.

The *real* fantasy most men harbour involves something more lethal. Like murder. Men plot countless murders during their lifetime. But mainly they dream about killing their bosses. Even if the boss happens to be a good guy who uses a deo and never raises his voice. Just the fact that he is boss is enough to make them feel murderous and uncontrollably violent. Wake up a man from a reverie and ask him the first thing on his mind. 'Oh hell—I thought I'd killed the bastard,' he'll murmur. And you won't need to know who the bastard is. Bosses figure big on men's hit lists. They represent everything the average Johnny would like to be. If the boss has a gorgeous wife, that instantly makes him an even more attractive target. It is when men are contemplating murder that their puny imaginations really soar. If you want to bond with your guy, pour yourself a large drink and discuss ways and means to castrate his boss ... before killing him off in some entirely unknown and deeply painful way.

But if you really are serious about bonding on this level with your mate, combine murder with sex. No—we aren't discussing necrophilia. Just marrying two very basic instincts. Men like the idea of harems . . . sex with multiple, exotic, veiled partners. Indulge them when they go into their Arabian Nights routine—and throw in the boss for the finale. Fling the swine to hungry lions in a gilded cage even as the man writhes in pleasure on velvet covers while sloe-eyed houris drape themselves over him, his eyes never leaving the hated creature being devoured nearby by those noble beasts. You're asking about your role in all this? Are you kidding? You are the one giving him great head while he dreams on.

Myths About Men

yth Number One: Men are Strong. We've all been raised on such myths. Lies. Damned lies. Forget the crap about the strong silent superman ready to shoulder all responsibilities. The guy who goes around playing Atlas is likely to be either a failed body-builder or Arnie Schwarzenegger himself. Men aren't strong. They are bullies. If they can possibly get away with their wives moving heavy furniture, carrying monstrous sling-bags while travelling (a kid on the other arm), pushing the car on a lonely highway—they will.

Take our noble peasants toiling in the fields. Who's doing the harder work? The women. Watch workers on a construction site—who hauls enormous stones over long distances? Not the men. Look around at airports. Who pushes the luggage trolley? Who gets bags off conveyor belts? Who then dangles one bambino on a jutted hip, while another kid clings to her knees? Who manages an overstuffed baby-bag holding nappies, bottles, portable potties? You've guessed right. And we've only just begun.

So much for Tarzan. Are men strong in the emotional department at least? Go take a long walk. They break faster under pressure. They whinge, whine and groan at the smallest provocation. They beg, plead and grovel without pride. They pass the buck deftly when all else fails. Their spines need fixing. So do their warped priorities.

Strong? That's a laugh.

In any crisis, it's the women who hang together. An accident site, a sudden death, failure in examinations, kidnapping, mugging, rape, abduction, surgery, elopement—the guys crumble. They play ostrich. Remove themselves from the scene. Act lofty and superior. Get drunk. The real stuff is invariably handled by the gals.

Myth Number Two: Men are Dependable. Baloney. Anybody who counts on a man to deliver the goods does so at her own peril. You can't possibly depend on a man, no way. They are either too busy (what with?), too rushed (where are they all going?), too tense (fuck—the rain has ruined another game of golf) or just too selfish (yup, that's closer to the truth). Ask a man to do something for you—something simple like pick up a jar of jam from the club for the kids. He'll come home without it. Ask for an explanation and he'll storm out of the house. Where is the bounder headed? Back to the club of course. To escape nagging. Will he remember to bring the jam this time? Don't count on it. But heaven help you if the laundry isn't accounted for. 'Where's my blue shirt?' he'll bellow as you get the mascara wand going half-an-hour before a party. 'Which blue shirt? The one you sent to the cleaners last week? Oh-oh. I forgot. It was meant to be ready today.' 'Forgot? You forgot my blue shirt? How could you? What do you expect me to wear now?' 'Well, darling, you have three dozen similar looking blue shirts—why not one of those?' 'Are you crazy? I don't want to wear one of those. I want to wear the one you forgot to collect from the laundry today. Forget it. We aren't going.'

Men don't write letters. They never thank anybody. And they do not remember special dates—like their children's birthdays. That's okay. Don't expect them to. If something has to be done on an anniversary or for a funeral, do it yourself. Unless you want to get involved in one of those pointless 'How the hell do you expect me to remember everything? I'm only a man' dialogues. Precisely, he's only a man.

Men can be one hundred per cent dependable, however, when it comes to meeting up with buddies at some favourite watering-hole. You can count on them to get out of your face when an old boozing partner breezes into town. Men will cancel anything—even postpone surgery—when that happens. Which is why guys find guys dependable. Women don't. Women know better.

Myth Number Three: Men are Dynamic. Are they really? They certainly want to be seen in that light. Turbo-charged chaps spinning around at dizzying speeds doing stuff. What stuff? Oh, they'll say dreamily—stuff. Guy stuff. Operating things that change the world. Putting up factories, going into space. Reassuring humans there's life on Mars after all. Going into battle. Designing frocks for rich ladies. Buying and selling companies. Getting people to spend money. That sort of stuff.

Well, all right. But does anybody really *need* all that?

Women do it differently. A dynamic woman (unless she is stupid enough to clone male behaviour) uses her energy to add quality to her own life and to the life of people around her. She looks into the future and works towards making it better. She gets her priorities right. She juggles her various (and varied) roles prudently. She loves. She enjoys sex. She flowers and flourishes. She chooses not to live on airplanes and catch up on life in transit lounges. She refuses to wear dull grey business suits. And she refuses to keep herself on hold while she attempts to solve the problems of the universe. Yes? Just as well.

Men are seen to be more dynamic only because men can afford to be more self-centred. They push ahead regardless once they've got their target in sight. This aspect of their personality has been given a pretty description of late. It is called the cutting edge. In the old days people were blunter about such things. Dynamic men living life on the cutting edge were called plain Ruthless Bastards. Today we refer to them as Captains of Industry.

Myth Number Four: Men are Born Charmers. They are?? Well—good for them. We could do with some charm around. However, it has been noticed that men who ooze charm are the same creeps who are trying to climb into as many knickers as they can. It's true that women are often taken in by this cheap trick. Charming the pants off a gal is easy. A slimeball knows that. And he doesn't have to be thirty-plus to master the art. I've seen similar operators starting early—real early. As early as ten or twelve. One can spot them easily—they're the brats with the winning smile and thick eyelashes. They're the ones who hang out with the girls at birthday parties and compliment them on their buckles and bows. It is these boys who grow up still hanging around girls and still laying on the superlatives. This isn't charm—this is goo.

Can women tell the difference? Rarely. Natural charm is charming because it is natural. (Huh? Read that again. It will make sense.) Very few men have it. They don't need to. Life is comfortable enough without it. Guys who go out of their way to acquire it expose themselves soon enough, but by then they've already travelled far in knicker-territory—which has been their prime priority all along.

Maurice Chevalier was charming. Maurice Chevalier *had* to be charming—that was his meal ticket. Plus, he didn't have the looks or talent to be successful any other way. Ashok Kumar is charming perhaps for the same reasons. It's the practised playboy-types who give charm a lousy name. Like a paunchy Mumbai wheeler-dealer who thinks it's cool to call lady bankers 'baby' while touching them for a loan. Put-on charm sucks. The genuine article sucks too, especially when there are strings attached.

Not every man can be an Omar Sharif. You can try, but do go easy on the bullshit, won't you? Dollops of charm are as icky as an overdose of gooey icecream. A couple of quick licks is all it takes to decide whether or not the entire scoop is worth swallowing. Besides, for some strange reason women associate smooth super-charmers with fairies. A good-looking guy who comes on a bit too strong with standard gush risks being dismissed as an insincere gay-boy out to steal your make-up—or worse, your husband.

Myth Number Five: Men are Ambitious. This is partly true. Men *are* ambitious. About all the wrong things. They want to get ahead in life, they say. They want nothing but the best. The want to conquer, to achieve, to move mountains, to discover new worlds, to go picnic on the moon, to bungee-jump from Mount Everest, Fine, fine, fine. But *puhleeze* leave us girls out of your lunatic agenda.

You want to move mountains, mate? That's okay by us. But how about moving the earth a little before you get into your trekking gear? Not exciting or challenging enough? That's exactly where you guys goof up. Ambition isn't about breaking records or jumping off cliffs. It is about getting it all together in a sane integrated way. It takes adventurers and assorted cranks to discover new vistas. But it also takes a few good men to keep our world from going out of control.

Women understand that instinctively. Ambition for most girls is defined by home and hearth—even corporate ladies prefer warm, occupied nests to chrome and glass cages. But men? They wish to defy biology itself. Besides, a lot of driven guys genuinely believe it is their ferocious appetite for 'getting there' that makes them irresistible to women. Somewhat true. Women don't mind going along for the ride. But they certainly don't want to stick around long enough to risk slipped discs over a bumpy road. Naked ambition often works as a complete turn-off. Fortunately, not too many guys have it. Why? Because the majority of them is simply too lazy to get off its butt and work hard enough for that pot of gold at the end of the rainbow. Fuck it, they mutter as they check the head on their beer. They kid themselves that to be truly successful a man has to be born under the right stars. 'It's all in your karma, yaar,' they slur over Singapore Slings as an acknowledged Take-Over king struts into the bar. 'That son-of-a bitch has good karma—that's all,' they console themselves, while the son-of-a-bitch gobbles up yet another company over cashewnuts and a soda. But ask these same fellows about their future plans and they'll talk in grandiose terms— deals, mergers, reorganizations, expansion plans. I mean, Warren Buffet could learn a trick or two if he stuck around. The big difference being Warren Buffet doesn't waste time on jerks. He doesn't faff around with losers. He is a real guy—and he does what a guy has to do, which is make money. Women love that. A man who is focused. Focused on putting his signatures on the right slips of paper. Not for them the average wimp who wilts at the sight of a bill in a fancy restaurant.

Most men fail to get it. They waste time discussing ambition instead of acquiring it. On the other side are the hopefuls—the innocents with ambition but zero abilities. The world is full of them. Which is why mediocrity rules. Never mind. If the man in your life seriously thinks he is Errol Flynn crossed with Bill Gates—with Akshay Kumar's sex appeal thrown in and a brain borrowed from Einstein for good measure—let him. Better that than a monkey on the hop. Men with burning ambition rarely have time for sex—it takes far too much time and effort. Besides, it cuts into their grand plan of getting ahead. So . . . if your sex drive is permanently in low-gear, go for the guy who heads for a powerful banker instead of a luscious starlet at a party. He'll never stray. He may never screw either. But that suits you just fine— doesn't it?

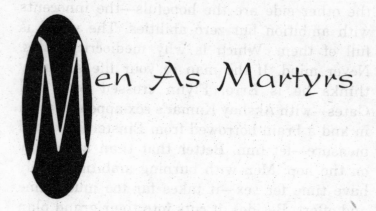

Men As Martyrs

No. No. No, guys. This role is reserved for women. Don't even think about auditioning for it. Martyrdom cancels out machismo. You don't want people feeling sorry for you, surely? People *love* feeling sorry for other people. Heck—don't you remember how delighted you were when your colleague broke a leg, didn't get his promotion, had to cancel his Caribbean cruise, couldn't get his son into school and flunked his club interview? You didn't exactly exchange high fives with the others and you were clever enough to conceal your thrill, but you *did* feel kinda glad to see the bugger moping all over the place or weeping silently onto his PC. 'What a jerk,' you sneered, as you strode around confidently, cracking jokes behind his back and displaying total concern face-to-face.

Men are sadistic creatures. They revel in other people's misfortunes. It makes them feel good about themselves. Superior. Tarzan-like. Even the puniest of guys strut around like Bionic Men when the chips are down—for someone else. Forget the empathy factor. Men don't know the meaning of that word. Empathy is seen as a 'girlie-thingie'. It's what women pretend to feel when their best friends appear with a ridiculous perm or a black eye. Men don't emphathize. They bond. Which, freely translated, reads: men booze.

Somehow, most men also realize instinctively that playing martyrs isn't sexy. Look what happened to poor Devdas. Tragic heroes have no real appeal except for a certain type of woman— the kind whose heart bleeds for a crushed autumn leaf, or who weeps at sundown because the poor sun is going away. Women who wipe crocodile tears off a cunning little urchin's face while he picks their pockets, are exactly the sort who flip for any man weeping into his whisky at a seedy bar. They richly deserve to be full-fledged, card-carrying members of the Martyrs' Club. Most regular girls shun these fellows. There is no pity worse than self-pity and when it comes with a proposition, it's the cheapest little trick in the world.

Martyred men follow a certain plan of action.

First they get you with their sob story. And then they try and bed you. The success rate isn't too bad either. And the odds are good—women who fall for this line are also willing to cook, clean and fuck for free. After all, they're feeling sorry for the guy. So sorry, that they can't wait to become his chattels. Most veteran martyrs wait for such a person to waltz along before turning on all the taps. Tears work—and work big— with our Bleeding Hearts. If the martyr plays his cards smartly enough, not only will the woman C, C and F for free, she'll also subsidize the ride by picking up all the bills even if it means she has to sell her jewellery and work two shifts somewhere. Does that shame the martyr? Are you kidding? This is the moment he has been preparing for. He cannot afford to show her there may be a spine to support that frame of his. The moment he sees her softening and/or reaching for her purse, he recognizes it as his cue to assume his best hangdog expression and let the tear ducts do their job. The old 'My-wife-doesn't-understand' or 'The-world-hates-me' route is a pretty well-travelled one. Several thick-skinned fellows have been on the Martyr Highway for life and cruised along comfortably enough.

Women who feel sorry for little birdies in their little nests, or puppies yelping on the sidewalk, gravitate towards these canny creatures and make them feel instantly better by merely listening to their tales of woe without guffawing. Martyrs are shrewd enough to know exactly how much to squeeze out of their personal tragedies—imaginary or real. When they see a woman getting a slightly glazed expression, they know it's time to switch to a more cheerful subject, like the colour of her eyes. Even the most hardened woman crumbles when some goofy no-good takes half-a-second off to say something dumb like, 'I didn't realize till this moment that you have the most amazing golden flecks in those eyes of yours. I could submerge myself in them forever.' How do you think Elizabeth Taylor agreed to marry all those jerks and even pay their orthodontists' bills? I'm pretty certain Larry Fortensky got into her life and bed by telling her about her violet eyes. And to think she'd probably been hearing the same silly lines about her incredible eyes ever since she was three years old. Did that make her immune to flattery? No. Did she ever tire of hearing the same sickening words about her uniquely coloured eyes? No. Does she still want to hear some more? Yes. Will she marry her physiotherapist/chauffeur/valet/laundry boy even today if he talks about her eyes? Yes, again. Women are real suckers in this department. Martyrs know it. They are men first and then martyrs, remember?

Sensible women stay miles away from martyrs. Sensible women can see through emotional conmen. Besides, they know a loser when they see one. And martyrs aren't all that difficult to spot—especially the saints who go around claiming they've given up everything for the sake of the social uplift of backward classes/ orphans/lepers/disabled canines/rape victims/the AIDS-afflicted. They've given up nothing at all, least of all a juicy subsidy. Yet, the coterie around these frauds tries to project them as selfless servants whose only desire is to give up their life for a cause. Actually, yes—that's partly true. The cause is generally themselves. And what have they actually given up? A low-paid job in some dump. It's a pretty neat trade-off considering the compensatory package—endless junkets to exotic destinations in developed countries to plead for their favoured charity. Lots and lots of moolah rolling in from all quarters to set up a hospital/school/orphanage/ centre. Hardly any accountability. Loads of publicity. in prestigious journals. Awards and accolades on national and international levels. Plus, some of the world's loveliest ladies ready to jump into bed with them—for the larger good of the chosen cause, of course. How can a social worker be effective if he is sexually frustrated, they reason. Think of the poor, deprived orphans and screw the man's brains out.

It's the same logic that makes women 'adopt' martyrs of different hues. They tell themselves, a suicidal fellow won't be allowed into heaven (and that's definitely his final destination) if he drowns himself in either severe depression or serious alcohol. The only way to save his soul (and get a roll in the hay too) is by feeding him—and feeding him well. Most professional martyrs develop hearty appetites once they meet their lady-patrons. They also get finicky and selective about their preferences. The same man who in the past has been happy enough with daal-chaval twice a day, now cannot swallow anything less than choice basmati rice cooked over a slow fire. He also develops an overnight taste for mutton pasanda and teetar. His palate rejects anything that doesn't came from a fine store. And naturally he can't drink army-quota rum any more, not when the woman is busy tapping all her sources to keep him in good Bourbon. He needs sustenance, she explains. After all, he is doing such good work. Yeah, you want to tell her, he sure is—on her.

Martyrdom as a career option is an excellent idea. And hugely profitable. Martyrs are generally good money-managers and weigh their gains in terms of tears shed. They know the value of their efficient lachrymal glands and look after their prized assets very well. Appropriate and convincing body language is the key to being a successful martyr. The stoop is important, so are the hunched-over shoulders and melancholy expression. Once the martyr masters all these he is ready and in business.

The ultimate martyr is the one who dies fighting some obscure but valiant battle. These chaps are usually crazy and pretty rare. But the world loves them anyway because the world generally approves of anybody who dies. Death confers instant respect.

Most ornery martyrs aren't willing to go quite this far to establish their credentials. Don't expect them to, either. It just isn't fair to insist that they die. But suffer they must. To be a bona fide martyr, one has to endure at least some degree of torture. It can come from a nag of a wife (the most common source), a tyrannical father, a no-good son, or a psychopathic boss. Only a man who can peddle personal torment in an attractive package can qualify as a martyr-to-be-taken-seriously. The rest are amateurs. If a woman must pick a Sad Sack, let him be a champion in his chosen field.

An obvious and visible physical disability goes a long way in tugging at a woman's heart-strings. Just a run-of-the-mill tic won't do. And if it's a hard-luck story involving theft, a terminal disease, deceit, heart-break, amputation, consumption—fine. It deserves to be milked. Anything less is pedestrian, and frankly, a bloody bore to boot.

Martyrdom's many guises require careful monitoring. If you are dying to play Florence Nightingale to some Suffering Soul, go right ahead after making sure the guy is really and truly suffering on a grand scale. A stubbed toe or an eczema patch does not a martyr make.

Do these guys qualify in the husband department? Depends. If you have a burning desire to sit around cooling fevered brows or warming cold beds in the hope that your love will transform everything—that's your decision. An insane one, I'd say. Otherwise, martyrs are better suited to being statues, monuments and samadhis. Not flesh-and-blood mates.

Men As Buddies

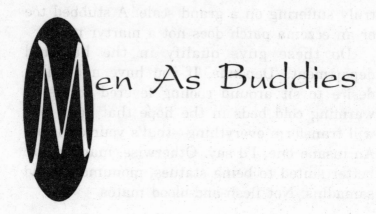

bout the only person ever to believe in platonic relationships was Plato himself. And even he probably realized he was conning the world. There are adherents to his philosophy who go around tying raakhis on the wrists of men they have anything but sisterly feelings for. The rationale? 'Oh . . . but we are platonic friends.'

Oh yeah?

This funny business of raakhi-brothers must be unique to India. The moment a young girl starts feeling a little dhak-dhak towards a young man (more often than not, her brother's best friend)—she decides to tie the knot. Only it isn't of the marital kind. This is where a raakhi is so handy. She tries to bond with the guy any which way she can, irrespective of his sentiments in the matter. Raakhis generate no guilt. Are affordable by all. Attractive too—even the garish, plastic-pink ones with tinsel fringes. And they allow two young people in a highly repressed society to talk to one another without the elders screaming 'rape'.

Raakhi-brothers are a dime-a-dozen in our society. People accept this odd arrangement. But nobody accepts male-female friendships ('They must be sleeping together' or 'If they aren't sleeping together now, they must've slept together at some point in the past'). The raakhi protects a woman from such charges and makes the relationship holy—sanctity being everything. Girls and boys can hold hands, flirt, go out, have fun, provided their relationship has been legitimized by a simple bracelet made out of coloured thread.

Buddies are harder to come by than raakhi brothers. Besides, can men and women ever be friends? Good friends? It's a dicey question. At some point there is a dangerous cross-over. At some point, one or the other flips and falls in love. At some point, someone generally spoils it all—a jealous spouse for example. 'What the hell do you see in that creep, anyway?' he might ask after you've giggled and lowered your voice on the phone once too often. 'What do you find to say to that nincompoop? He's such a bloody bore. An asshole, really, if you must know.' That's the signal. Once those words are uttered, your relationship is finished. Kaput. Doomed. Even if you have grown up with the guy and gone to kindergarten together. Maybe you share a passion. Could be Tchaikovsky, Bhimsen Joshi, lemon grass, bird-watching, porno films, cooking low-cal mush, deep sea diving, dog-walking, stealing menu cards—that sort of stuff. But if the activity excludes the spouse, your buddy is dead meat.

It cuts both ways. A suspicious wife can look daggers at a woman her husband insists he has nothing but pure *ganga jal* feelings for since they'd both been army kids stuck at a remote outpost in the back of beyond while their respective daddies defended the motherland. Will she understand and call the woman over for coffee and cake? Are you kidding? Her imagination will go into instant over-drive as she starts visualizing the two of them making kinky, adolescent love in an army jeep on a remote highway in Arunachal Pradesh. That's it. That's where they must've done it, she'll conclude. It's the ideal locale for a hot affair. She won't say that outright and get it over and done with. She will wait for a week and then raise the subject with her unsuspecting husband when he's least expecting her to. Like, say, when he's about to crack the crossword. Or is talking to his lawyer about a huge settlement in a long-pending case. Or while he's busy powdering the fungus between his toes, or there's an income-tax raid on and he's being grilled by a sadist with stained teeth. At precisely such a moment, she will turn to him viciously and say, 'Tell me another. As if I don't know you were screwing Meera.' The poor fellow won't know who the fuck Meera is at that point, since she doesn't really figure in his life except in an affectionate, distant sort of way. Naturally, he'll look blankly at his wife and ask, 'Who's Meera?' She'll pounce on him (yes—in front of all those income-tax guys) and yell triumphantly, 'I *knew* you'd say that. I just knew it. Well, you can't fool me. I know all about you and her. I bet she seduced you when both your dads were posted in Meghalaya. Admit it, you coward.' The husband will look helplessly at the raiding party and shrug. They'll look back with a sympathetic, 'All women are completely dotty' expression. Even at a time like that, the men will bond. Handcuffs may follow later. But the brotherhood of that moment will be as real as the charge-sheet they'll soon be framing.

Women find it hard enough to establish emotional links with other women—daughters, sisters and mothers included. To expect them to accept their natural enemies (men) as buddies, is to be both unrealistic and overly optimistic. Women can sometimes just about tolerate the opposite sex. But friendship and fellow-feeling?

Nyet. Nyet. Under truly extraordinary circumstances, perhaps. Or when survival itself depends on it. Like say, a mixed group decides to scale a mountain and the woman's nose gets frost-bitten. The men in the group will feel for her and do something about it—like bite the useless thing off. Or take the case of female astronauts sharing a constricted space with manic-looking Russian men. The girls don't have even a powder room to call their own. And as if that isn't bad enough, they can't switch outfits, or even flirt from behind those ugly plastic bubbles covering their faces. With such horribly limited options, they do the next best thing—make friends with the Russkies and organize frequent vodka-breaks with some caviar thrown in.

The fact of the matter is, men don't really like women all that much. In a word-association game, men are likely to come up with the following: 'whores'; 'harlots'; 'ingrates'; 'treacherous two-timing bitches'. Women don't get this carried away when asked to return the compliment. They have one word that covers it all: 'farts'.

Indian women are conditioned from an early age to place men in three well-defined categories. Father, brother and husband. The question of friendship doesn't arise. Adult women do not have independent, one-on-one relationships with men unless they're sleeping with them—or intend to at some point in the future. Unless the men happen to be self-acknowledged gays. Even then, a woman can take the relationship no further than a few lunches and phone calls a year. 'How do you know he's gay?' her enraged partner will demand after overhearing a particularly giggly exchange. The woman may say mysteriously, 'I just know.' But that won't be explanation enough. 'I must say the "gay" label is a very convenient one these days,' the man might sneer. And a fight will follow. 'My foot he's gay. Don't think I'd didn't notice him pawing you at the Popli party. Bloody pervert. All these queers are alike—give them an inch and they go for your boobs.' Note: not balls. Boobs.

Women keen to break into a straight men's club will soon find the guys closing ranks and shutting her out. If she tries being 'one of the boys' (à la Shirley Maclaine and the Hollywood Rat Pack), she might land in even deeper trouble. Women are seen as nosey intruders with nothing to contribute in any area that doesn't fall directly under 'sex'. I've observed hard-drinking, cigar-chomping ladies matching a group of men peg for peg at a bar. More often than not, they've submerged their own identity to become slightly comical clones of the chaps knocking back the beer. Women who try too hard, who swear and cuss, who hunt big game, wear rugged clothes, deepen their voices, pump iron, drive jeeps, grow moustaches—in other words, do everything possible to mimic what they consider 'male' behaviour—generally end up alone and feeling foolish.

Aversion to female company starts early in a male's life. Watch any group of little boys as they spin tops, shoot marbles or sit passively in front of a TV set. Note their reaction when a little girl walks in and tries to join them. At first they'll pretend she's invisible. If ignoring her doesn't work, they'll whisper rude things about her between themselves. If she continues to hang around, they'll shove her off the sofa. If none of this has the desired effect on Ms Thick-Skin, they'll stop whatever they're doing, split up and head off in different directions.

Does the little girl get the message and vow never to face such humiliation again? No. She tries even harder as she grows older. Because the poor thing genuinely believes it's possible to be friends with boys—whatever their age.

Boys are far clearer about this. No broads. That's it. No wonder they form all sorts of secret societies from which females are strictly excluded. They need protection and privacy. The only way to get those is by keeping women out—physically, if they have to. Women, being shameless and rhino-skinned, never stop hoping. Do they ever get it? Rarely, if at all. They still want to crash the party.

It is nothing more than nosiness that makes them behave in such an obnoxious manner.

Sensitive creatures (like dogs) realize when they aren't wanted and slink away to hide their humiliation. Not women. They nag husbands into taking them along to meet the boys, knowing all the while their presence is going to annoy everybody—husbands included. Men cannot indulge in man-talk if there's even one woman hanging around to spoil it all. Man-talk consists of nothing more significant than bragging and bitching. Yes, bitching. Men love to stick the bitch-tag on to us girls, but sorry, guys, in the female canine stakes, you win hands down.

So the logical question to ask is, if men bitch anyway and they are convinced it's women who bitch, why can't the sexes join up and bitch together? It doesn't work out somehow. There are gender issues involved and the bitching doesn't quite synchronize either subject-wise or time-wise—unless there's a common target—and even in those circumstances men often spoil all the fun by adopting a sanctimonious, holier-than-thou attitude—right after tearing the victim to shreds and stomping all over the remains. If women have participated in the slaughter, they are the ones who're stuck with the blame for 'starting the gossip in the first place'. Irrespective of who had initiated the character assassination, at the end of the bloody session, when post-mortems are conducted, all the men will gravitate to one side, point fingers at the women and chorus, 'Bitches.' They'll throw in the usual clichés too. Like, 'Never tell a woman what you don't want the entire world to know.' 'Heard the latest joke? Some jerk actually trusted a female. Isn't that funny?' 'Let's tape all future conversations. That way we'll be able to prove to the women that it was they who did the bitching. We only listened. What were we supposed to do? Cover our ears?'

Men as buddies did exist in Hollywood films of the '40s and '50s. But even in those, the dividing line between buddyship and lovers was not clearly defined. Stars as antiseptic as Fred Astaire and Ginger Rogers invariably started out as friends in their films together, and ended up in, if not the proverbial bed, then at the altar as man and wife. Not man and female buddy. Nope. It doesn't work. Women expect emotional reassurance from friendship. Men demand loyalty—unswerving loyalty. The definition itself has a different interpretation for the sexes. Is anybody really complaining? Men can keep their buddies. Real babes prefer lovers.

Men As Mice

You find them cute? You think they're harmless little rodents, scurrying around in search of cheese? Maybe you're right. But girl—do you see yourself as that piece of Brie? Besides, rodents have sharp little teeth that bite. You don't want a rodent-bite. In fact you don't want a rodent-anything.

There are men who are mice. And men who play at being mice. That's okay. We are smart enough to recognize the difference. Men who suffer from a serious identity crisis and go around behaving like little grey critters deserve to be treated likewise. Some women prefer to stand on the nearest chair and shriek 'eek' at the sight of the genuine article. Especially women in cartoons. But men who are mice elicit a different response altogether—women feel like picking up that same chair and breaking it over the chap's head. A mighty roar in his general direction also helps. But beware: a mouse is generally attached to something larger and fiercer—his mother. In fact, the reason he is a mouse is her although one suspects some men are born mice and stay that way. If you've kept a small, furry pet, say, a hamster, as a child, this is the man for you. He demands very little and is happy enough with the few scraps you throw in his direction. He also lets you do your own stuff without a squeak. Which means, if you are a power babe in the fast-track and your job involves a great deal of travel at short notice—be happy you have this nice-mice person willing to stay home and look after the kiddies.

Mice are generally good to have around at parties as well—they don't make a noise, fix drinks surprisingly well, peck at the canapes, rarely ogle other people's wives, behave decorously and best of all—pay for everything. Mice make dependable husbands. Rich mice in particular. If you find a mouse with a huge inheritance—grab him. He is generally good with his money and generous too. You might want to run through all that lolly in a hurry before dumping the mouse—but forget it. Behind that mousey exterior is a shrewd mind that is fully aware of your wicked game plan.

Male mice rarely marry their female counterparts. They prefer tigresses. Why so? Well, tigresses make them look less like mice in the eyes of the world. People stupidly conclude that a man who is with a dynamite lady couldn't be a complete zero. They begin to fantasize that maybe he is a dynamite lover in bed. A man who has mastered a few clever tricks. Someone who knows which buttons to press and when. Baloney. But this mouse is smart, he *knows* that's exactly what you are imagining. And he is delighted to let you go on imagining it. The logical question to ask in that case is, what does the tigress do for entertainment and sexual pleasure? Generally, she goes in search of a tiger . . . maybe the office peon. The mouse doesn't mind. How can he? He's a realist. He knows he can't possibly match his appetite with his wife's. It's part of their deal. Mice seem to go for flamboyant, exhibitionistic women in a big way—they figure a high-visibility, colourful partner adds a li'l something to their own invisibility. People actually look to see who the fabulous babe is with—and the mouse gets noticed.

Do not underestimate mice though. They are inconspicuous enough to go completely unnoticed—and that is where their power lies. Yes, their wives break rules flagrantly. Yes, their kids treat them like turds. Yes, their business partners push them around. And yes, they are consistently ignored by maitre d's all across the globe. Aha—that's when the mouse strikes. Mighty Mouse. When you least expect it. Remember, even elephants have problems with these pests. So does poor Tom when Jerry decides enuf is enuf. Mice are capable of great cunning when their little hole (sorry, but that is exactly what a mouse's abode is called) is threatened. With ingenuity and stealth, the mouse strikes back and even woman hath no fury like a mouse scorned.

The trickier mouse is the one who's *playing* at being one, usually because of a striking physical resemblance to the lowly rodent. This is the one who pretends to respond to the Pied Piper while plotting all along to gnaw right through the Piper's jock-strap to chew up his testicles. It's hard to isolate and identify this species. The pretend mouse is generally a puny specimen with mean, darting eyes that miss nothing. Underestimate him and you do so at your own risk. Being small in size but often large on ego, this mouse moves in mysterious ways. He gets around disarming adversaries with a deceptively meek manner. He may have a booming voice but he rarely employs it. When he chooses to bellow, the impact is impressive ('Wow, so much lung power in that miniscule chest'). Power is a big turn-on for this guy since his presence so lacks it. He relishes the trappings of it, however, and plays for tough stakes. You can spot him at a pre-Diwali gambling evening—he's the chap with the biggest stack of notes. He makes up in cash what he sorely lacks in personality. But don't mess with him—he can chew you up, one painful bite at a time.

The big mouse is easier to handle. This is one large, miserable blob of low self-esteem. Who knows what his private demons are (a tiny ding-dong? Abused childhood? Sibling rivalry? Impeded locomotion? Bad breath?). The man is a sitting duck waiting to be shot. Dull, slow, uninspiring, the woman with him is likely to be equally drab. You expect the mouse couple to arrive in a mousemobile, not a Maruti. But there they are, whiskers quivering inquisitively, beady eyes scouring the room. Try making mousetalk—discuss sewage, dengue, sanitation. The mouse couple will display few signs of actual animation. Don't be entirely deceived by the facade however. Some male mice can outperform stud horses in bed. They can also be wife-beaters and abusive bullies. Watch them scamper around near the boss' boots and you'll get the picture. The smaller the mouse, the meaner his temper. The big mouse is comparitively harmless—unless he turns into a vicious bandicoot, a sewer rat. Watch out for him then, for he'll go after you in a manner even you will find impossible to counter. Keep him out of your bed at all costs—he may chew up your linen along with bits and pieces of your arm, thigh and neck. Men who resemble and or behave like garden rats should be treated likewise—poisoned pellets generally do the trick quite effectively. Knead some into the chappati dough and feed the fellow lovingly. Better still, burn him with the garbage—we don't need another outbreak of the dreaded plague. Just make sure your environment is mice-proof. Don't act like melting Camembert . . . or smell like rancid Kodi cheese. You never know with men (or mice). Everything smells of sex to them. Even mouldy cheese.

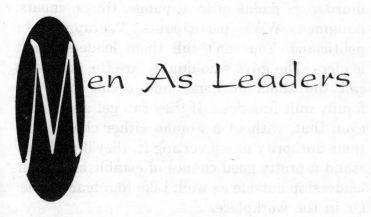

Men As Leaders

Remember how we grew up on Alpha Male theories? Remember buying them unquestioningly? Remember calling your father that in disparaging terms? And believing you were hurling the worst possible insult at him? Remember also that all the men you knew aspired to be Alphas, because they seriously believed chicks only went for that type?

Guess what? Chicks like 'em any which way—alphas, betas, whatever. It's true that some males display alpha traits the moment they kick their mothers real hard while still in the womb, but these males are exceptions with an abnormally high level of testosterone floating around in their systems. They grow up to be murderous dadas of local gangs, thugs, cheats, hangmen, WWF participants, Veerappans or politicians. You can't call them leaders. Legit leaders. The guys who qualify are the ones who call the shots at home and decide how the family unit functions. If they can get away with even that, without a woman either challenging their authority or subverting it, they'll probably stand a pretty good chance of establishing their leadership outside as well. Like in a team game. Or in the workplace.

Real leaders are pretty easy to spot. They generally wear a large sign around their necks that reads 'Leader'. You may wish to ignore it or snigger at it. But a guy who has the gall to sport such a sign probably means business when it comes down to brass-tacks. Don't mess with him, particularly not if he is your boss/husband or both. Fathers who fancy themselves as leaders are easier to manipulate. All you have to do is let them think they're hot shit—that's what they want to believe. And that's generally enough to keep them off your back. Husbands, who not only think they're leaders but also want to behave like them, are harder to crack. But it's possible. Provided you know which screws to tighten. Which to ignore. Which to unscrew altogether. Assertive husbands can be easily and effectively trained to become purring pussycats while still hanging on to their leader-label. It takes time and patience but it's well worth the effort. The same is not true about bosses. The difference? It's easier to be sacked by a boss who feels you are threatening his position as leader than be divorced by a husband who feels likewise. Any experiments you wish to conduct in this area should first be attempted at home. Wait sufficiently to assess the repercussions. And proceed cautiously thereafter.

People say Rajiv Gandhi was a good leader of men. *Was* he? That softie with his spaniel eyes? Let's give him the benefit of the doubt. He was perceived as a good leader of men only because he was his mother's son. Period. And *she* was perceived as an iron-fisted leader of people. It was leadership through association—it just rubbed off on the guy. It's possible that he grew into the role and loved it so much he decided, 'What the hell. It feels so good. Why don't I just go for it?'

Bill Clinton oozes oodles and oodles of the stuff of leadership. And so charmingly packaged, one doesn't notice the knife in the water . . . err . . . the knife in the paw. Women (and maybe a few misguided men too) would gladly follow him to the ends of the world if he so much as crooked his little finger at them. He has it all—good looks, charisma, a great smile, super body language and the unbeatable ability to press flesh very convincingly, very undiscriminately indeed. It helps. Plus, people secretly admire him for having survived a terminator called

Hillary. Any man who can share a bed with someone as formidable can survive nuking. Hillary prepared her man to take it all in his stride—the presidency, the publicity, the panic-attacks and the hand-shaking sessions with Yeltsin.

Do leaders make good husbands? Good fathers? Good lovers? Good sons? Good anythings? Or is leadership to be seen in isolation—as a by-product of the system? Like say . . . a train needs a good engine-driver and who cares whether or not he goes down on his wife as often as she'd like him to. He keeps the train on the track—right? And that's what defines him, his professional life. Similarly, it's irrelevant whether Bill keeps track of Hillary's menstrual cycle or whether he monitors Chelsea's high school grades. He gives inspiring speeches. And according to Gennifer Flowers, he gives good head too. America seems to be solidly behind him. That's all that matters in the election year. He can keep his bimbos and his scams. Who cares about Whitewater? The man is a leader. People are supposed to look up to leaders. Follow them. Emulate them. Not psychoanalyse their behaviour or be judgemental.

Do women find leaders sexy? Does power turn them on? Yes. Oh, yes. Any piddling leader can snap his fingers and get the girls. Even a local talukdar. Women worship influential people. Walk into a general post office and notice the look of naked power in the eyes of even the lowliest postal clerk. The one who can close down a counter in seconds. The one you've queued up in front of for forty-five minutes. Look exasperated or disappointed and he will walk away for a lunch break of unspecified duration. But look pleadingly into his eyes, beseech him to have mercy, grovel at his feel, and the puny fellow will start resembling Arnie in *Eraser*. He'll actually look monumental, great and strong as he grunts in your direction, accepts your money and slips a few stamps through the window. If stamps is what you require on a regular basis, you need to cultivate this swine. Given time, this same swine will start looking good in your eyes. Only because he has the power to cut down on or increase your waiting time in front of his insignificant counter.

It's the same with the classic boss-secretary office affair. In the eyes of the secretary, the boss is an invincible mighty, omnipotent, god-like creature who has the capacity to remote-control the lives of his or her minions. That makes the person unbelievably (and often, unrealistically) sexy. Promotions, perks, out-of-turn loans—everything is possible because The Leader likes you. Women by and large suffer from low self-worth. They rarely see themselves as powerful, even when they have unimaginable wealth and/or influence. Look at what happened to Christina Onassis, for example. Women do not associate the word 'power' or 'leadership' with themselves. The reference point is always men. In yet another word-association game, both these terms are likely to generate responses such as: 'Hitler'. 'Napoleon'. 'Stalin'. 'Mussolini'. Why? Because fear is the key.

Power induces fear. Leaders have to be feared first, revered later. Mahatma Gandhi's name is not likely to be the first one to come to mind even though he, more than almost any other individual, influenced the largest mass of people. Because nobody was afraid of him. Nobody felt threatened by him. That's why nobody found him sexy. Whereas, Jinnah was sexy. Leadership without a hint of menace, power lacking in sting or bite, that's not potent at all. Women really flip out on the accessories of power and leadership. Guns. Nuclear subs. Air Force One. Black Cats. AK-47s. Rashtrapati Bhavan. 10, Janpath. Fatwas. They love the pomp and circumstance. The whole shebang.

However, power without visible perks is worthless. What is the point of having it all if nobody benefits? Power requires a platform. Every leader needs a theatre, a mesmerized audience. Power is about performace. And applause. Leaders and the led.

Women, unfortunately, see themselves as the led. It's only the exceptional female who leads naturally, instinctively, without bringing gender into the picture. Which is why one can count the female world leaders on the fingers of a single hand. More often than not they are women who are there because their slain husbands have left attractive widows (them!) behind for canny generals to pick up and place like puppets on the seat of power. Diffidence goes with the male concept of femininity and most women prefer to play the shrinking violent role rather than risk alienation. Desperate for men's approbation, they willingly play down the assertive aspects of their personality while playing up the helpless angle.

It certainly works a whole lot better than the bulldozer approach. Women are better able to lead other women. When it comes to calling the shots in a mixed situation, they tend to either feign submissiveness or turn into fearsome ball-breakers on a rampage. There are no winners here. Men hate them. And women hate them too. Moral of the story: let men play that crummy role. It has no real rewards. As for us, girls, we'd rather settle for the spin-offs of being a king's/dictator's/general's wife . . . or main squeeze.

Surviving

Men

Men And Timing

Every women knows the Golden Rule in marriage: wait for the right timing. Men are very particular about it. If the woman gets her timing wrong, finished. She has blown it. Sometimes, forever. Timing is everything—even if it happens to be totally off as far as she's concerned. Who said anything about asking her, anyway? The woman discovers early on in the game that if she mistimes something even as inconsequential as an innocent query ('What would you like for dinner?') the man is likely to curse/spit/kick/stomp his foot/or march off, banging the front door shut behind him.

A smart woman becomes an even smarter one when she graduates to being a full-time face-reader. She is the one with the mood-meter in her hand. If she misreads the moment and gets the signals mixed up, well then, that's her funeral. Men are most concerned with trivial matters like the right timing. Especially when they're boot-licking the boss and asking for a raise. Then they turn into instant experts and know how to interpret the mysteries of a boss' smallest scowl. At home, the story is slightly different. The man bellows, the woman submits. If she has something of enormous personal significance to convey (e.g., 'Darling, I got the biopsy results. It's cancer'), she must realize that she cannot just blurt it out the minute he walks in (after a hard day crammed with important work). No. If she is astute, she must wait. The wait could stretch from anything between two minutes to two years, but wait she must. Small anxieties, of course, have to be dealt with solo, not involving the Big Boy (who has better, far more important matters to see to—like the Saturday night card game).

Men don't like to be confronted with what they call 'women's problems'. These include mastectomies, deaths in her family, hair loss, weight gain, hysterectomies, assorted fractures, unwashed laundry, wine stains, children's traumas, hospitalization. With the exception of his car, everything else at home falls under the 'nothing major' category. Heaven help you if the car is included in a crisis—any crisis. The first

questions a man is likely to ask when you call
tearfully to say that you're paralysed neck down
and speaking from the intensive care unit of the
hospital are, 'But what about the car? Is it
dented? Could someone have pinched the
hubcaps while you were unconscious?' Once
reassured that the car is just fine and no, all the
hubcaps were there when the ambulance arrived,
he might remember to add conversationally, 'Oh
well, then. I guess everything's all right. By the
way—how are you? Nothing serious I hope?' You
manage to whisper hoarsely, 'I'm fine. Really. At
least I can move my eyeballs. So far. The doctor
says he can't tell about tomorrow. Other than
that, yes, I'm fine. But don't worry too much
about the car. We are covered. I checked the
insurance papers on the way to the hospital.
And don't worry about me. I'll be okay. You go
right ahead and attend the boss' dinner party. I
won't mind.' The man instantly cheers up. 'Great,
I think I'll do that. Have you remembered to
wrap the present I bought him? No? Damn. I'll
have to do it myself. Really—a man asks a small
thing of his wife—but does she remember?' By
then, your IV drip may be running dry. You
may feel life oozing out of you. Do you enrage
your already annoyed husband by telling him?
Of course not. You apologize instead, for
forgetting the gift and other transgressions. Your
eyes are shutting with fatigue. The pain is
numbing you. But you tell yourself not to cry

and irritate him with your 'weaknesses'. He can't stand tears. Besides, he must be getting late for the party. See? All a question of timing.

If you aren't dead by the next morning, and he remembers there was no wife in his bed the previous night, he may just show up at the hospital looking bright and bouncy. 'How are we doing?' he'll ask, without too much interest. Then he'll pick up the strips of medication and pretend to read them intently. Actually he's buying time and figuring out what to say. If he's at all sheepish or apologetic, he'll conceal it behind bluster and silly bonhomie. You, of course, will be busy studying his face for signs of irritation before opening your mouth to say, 'Excuse me . . . I really hate to bother you, knowing how busy you are with the board meeting, but I do require a life-saving drug. Is it too much trouble to ask your brother to send it from the States?' His expression will alter immediately, darkening as he looks at you with an annoyed frown. 'You *know* my brother is vacationing in Florida right now. He *always* vacations in Florida at this time of year. Can't the damned drugs wait till he gets back? If you insist I can always disturb him at the resort . . . but if you ask me, I think it's a bloody nuisance.'

You give in weakly and pray that you don't die before his board meeting or else he'll have you to blame for the deal falling through ('See . . . she couldn't even die at a convenient time. It had to coincide with my meeting. It's just my bad luck. Something to do with my past life's sins'). By then, the man is tapping the toe of his well-polished shoe and admiring himself in his reflection (the one in the glass pane, not the one in the mirror). You notice he has dressed with more care than usual and has used far too much cologne (yours??). You catch him looking at his watch. Your breathing is shallow and sharp, but you don't want to alarm him (that is, in case he has noticed). So you wave him away, and smile a pained smile. He thinks you are worried about the car and assures you, 'It wasn't all that bad. The garage has given the estimate. I thought it would be much more. Of course it needs a paint job—but that was overdue, anyway. Don't look like that. I'm not angry. Really. I was expecting something horrendous. Sixty-seventy grand, minimum. The other good news is the garage-owner said he'll return it within a week—great, huh? I thought I'd be carless for a month.' It's your case to point out that the accident took place with the second car. The family car. Not his precious Cielo. He nods pleasantly and exclaims, 'Yes, thank God! Can you imagine what would have happened if you'd banged *that* one up?'

Of course you can imagine. That one might've cost you your life, while with this one you got away with mere paralysis.

He looks at his watch again and straightens

his tie. 'Well—time to go. Need anything?' You shake your head and say, 'Nothing.' You even manage a tender, wifely look (through the bandages) as you say, 'Good luck at the presentation. Do well.' He is out of the door before you can complete your sentence. Your head lolls over. The nurses think you are dead. Not on your life, you want to tell them. Not today. It's his board meeting. Bad timing.

Women are not supposed to have any priorities whatsoever—unless they revolve around the men in their lives. A personal agenda of a woman's own? No way. Not unless she wants to be branded a selfish, self-centred bitch. Personal goals occasion equal displeasure. Unless these include sacrifice on a major scale and preferably, compromises on time and energy, a woman risks losing the love of her partner. He will accuse her of not having enough 'space' for him and his needs in her life.

A *man's* personal goals are different. They're what define him. He is called dynamic and ambitious because he has them. A woman's primary concern is to nurture these goals like precious blossoms and provide a supportive environment for them to flower in.

A sense of timing is crucial when it comes to women announcing their little plans and projects. Say a woman has just been awarded some top honour; the equivalent of the Bharat Ratna; the Nobel; the Prix Goncourt; the order of the British

Empire. Does she go dancing to her husband with the news? Does she spontaneously pick up the phone and exult? Does she book a table for two in anticipation of the celebration ahead? No. Not unless she wants to get her head blown off. Sensibly and coolly, she waits. And she tries to figure out the best time to break the news to him. Before or after dinner? Now or later? Straight off, or should the ground be prepared first? Announce it with a triumphant smile, or play the whole thing down? Look thrilled or pretend it's no big deal? So many anxieties to figure out before booking her passage!

Not so in a man's case. Something good happens and there he is on a rooftop crowing about it. Does he wait for his wife to come back from a family crisis? Does he care if one of the kids has just been picked up on a drugs charge? Does he notice that his mother-in-law has died that very afternoon? Of course not. The first thing he does is fax the news to his worst enemies (the friends come later). Then he pours himself a large drink, sits back and puffs out his chest while waiting for the congratulations to pour in. The wife gets to know by and by but she's kept on 'call waiting' while he profusely thanks the man who'd sacked him seventeen years earlier. The celebrations come soon after, with the wife slaving in the kitchen while he backslaps his buddies at the bar.

Business trips? Hey—that's simple. A man

just picks up his bags and leaves. What does his female counterpart do? For starters, she prays. Once she has unburdened herself to God, she starts thinking about the timing. Should she phone him at the office and just say it out loud? Nope. Bad move. After taking all possible factors into consideration, she decides to wait till after dinner (generally considered an auspicious time even by astrologers). Once in bed (he with his financial papers, she with her paperback), she brings up the topic of her important trip. At first he pretends he hasn't heard her and starts discussing the mega merger he's reading about even though it has nothing to do with their lives. Then he shushes her because there is an earth-shaking piece of news on TV—scientists in Turkistan have discovered a cure for ant-bite. Finally he turns to her (after going to the loo and flossing his teeth for twenty minutes) and asks, 'So . . . you were saying?' By then she has died half-a-dozen times over and decided not to make the trip after all. She has even written the letter declining the offer in her mind and rehearsed the speech she'll make the next day when the boss calls her in.

Women who work at home have it even worse. Nobody takes them seriously, not even the servants. Men think nothing of interrupting them. Children show scant respect. And others? Heck—if the husband thinks so little of what his wife is doing, she must be doing it all wrong—right? Women who are lunatic enough to work out of their houses deserve the contempt they earn. The workplace is sacred. The dining table is not—that's where the family eats. Never confuse the office with the bedroom. You are asking for trouble—and you'll get plenty of it too. In today's commercial world a woman who doesn't bring in any lolly is a liability—plain and simple. Men do not hesitate to point that out in explicit terms. If she power-dresses, picks up her mobile and rushes out at ten past nine (timing it perfectly, so that her husband has to butter his own toast), he'll beam with pride and introduce her as 'the boss' at the next cocktail party. If she hangs around in a crumpled house frock with untidy hair and a frazzled expression, he'll treat her worse than the maid who has burnt his favourite shirt. The family will push her around and expect her to fetch and carry, because they are busy with 'important' things— while she is only a housewife committed to caring for them. No wonder women who stay home go around with such hangdog expressions these days. What choice do they have?

Aha, but women who make the big bucks at a swanky office—now, they're the ones who tell the family exactly when and where to get off. Does anybody protest? Not a chance. Men feel overawed by visibly successful ladies.

Men are also overawed by lipstick. If the visibly successful ladies also know how to apply their favourite shade expertly, men will fall like flies around their feet—and stay there waiting to be swatted. Or crushed under their pencil-thin heels. Lipstick connotes glamour and power. A woman who keeps her lips naked is asking to be devalued. No matter what her other achievements are—no lipstick means no power. (Children are impressed by lipstick as well. And perfectly manicured nails.) A fiercely well-groomed woman may intimidate people by her presence, but nobody will dare to tell her to untie a shoelace, pack sandwiches, remember to collect the laundry, cancel a dentist's appointment, change a tyre, summon a plumber or climb on a high stool to retrieve something heavy from a loft. No siree. Men (husbands included) will rush to open doors, buy her sexy lingerie, admire her cooking (lousy as it is) and sniff her new fragrance with eyes shut, while she works on her papers, watches BBC's *Business Hour* and gives the p.c. a good work-out.

On the other hand, the poor fool who stays home slaving for her family gets the wrong end of the stick all her miserable life. Her husband calls impatiently, 'Hey, you. Water. Cold—but no ice.' Children stop noticing her existence after their bellies are full and they have friends over. Even her husband's colleagues treat her like abandoned baggage and demand samosas while they sit around chatting in the living room. Nobody thinks anything of disturbing her at odd hours and demanding unrealistic favours. After all, she isn't doing 'anything'. Translated: she isn't contributing to the family kitty. But even if she is, by quietly embroidering organdie serviettes and selling them to a select few, she is still not taken seriously because she's around all the time—on call twenty-four hours of the day.

Does this woman ever rest? Is she allowed to put her feet up? Take some time off for herself? Binge on a shopping spree? Never. No concessions. And certainly no indulgence for her. Guilt is what permanently defines her state of mind. She is guilty because she isn't earning enough for her family to respect her time and priorities. And she's guilty because she isn't doing enough even if she is stopping just short of giving her life for the ingrates who surround her. Emergencies, big and small, are automatically hers to handle. The husband cannot be disturbed. He has meetings and appointments. He deals with VIPs. He pays the bills. Why involve him in petty issues like a fracture, or a gas cylinder explosion in the kitchen? What's the woman there for? If their teenage son is feeling suicidal and has threatened to leap off the sixteenth floor—leap off, not bungee-jump—that's the mother's concern. It's her department. If the daughter's doctorate is being noticed in academic circles—well, that's different. After all, daddy was the one who put her in touch with the right people. And mummy? Hmmm—she kind of helped. She stayed up nights sorting out papers. She kept the other children out of the genius' hair. She soaked almonds for her to chew on each morning. She took care of the calls. And, oh yes, she keyed in the whole thesis when it was done. But that's about all. Nothing major. No, nothing *major*. It never is.

Men find it difficult to be generous when it comes to acknowledging the contribution women make to their lives. When men talk in clichés (which is frequently) such as 'Behind every successful man . . .', they talk in a tone that is half-jocular—just in case some women take things seriously and demand a piece of the action for themselves. Such statements are made to keep women quiet—at least temporarily. 'See . . . I told everybody at the office party that my promotion was thanks to you. What more do you want? A citation?' A woman is grateful even for something as small and phoney as that cliché. She simpers and glows while people look upon her kindly, even though what they're really thinking is, 'Silly bitch.'

Women, on the other hand, seem over eager to attribute their own success to the first man in their immediate vicinity—generally, the father— later, a boss. And finally, the husband, who accepts the accolades without so much as a blush.

Men take the credit for everything—that's just the way they are. If a kid does well at school, it's because he or she is *his* kid. If the wife excels as say, a painter of oils, it's because *he* has provided her an inspiring environment. If a junior at work scrambles up the corporate ladder it is because the boss has encouraged him. Men even bask in the glow of a women's natural beauty, and somehow link it up with their contribution to it. *Contribution?* Yup. Stuff like, 'It's because of the good sex I provide, that your skin glows.' The key words being 'I' and 'provide'—like a home-delivery pizza service or something. A clever woman indulges such meaningless remarks and smiles back sweetly. What does it cost her if it makes the chest-thumping male next to her feel smug and wonderful? Better a smug and wonderful-feeling partner than a competitive, insecure brute. Ask any super successful woman and she'll tell you that it helps her sanity to keep the men around her on her side. So, with such opposing views on timing and excellence, can men and women ever be friends? Well we've been into that already. Think about what I said. Meanwhile, watch how differently the two eat bananas or grapes. It says a lot.

How To Train Men

Really girls—this one is easy. Simple. No one has to tell us what to do. We kinda *know*. We've watched our mothers in action since we were little girls. And we picked up all the cues as we went along. In so many different and endearing ways, men are like donkeys. They operate on an elementary reward-and-punishment level. A clever woman knows when to offer what—the old carrot-and-stick routine. Problems arise when she mixes up the order and offers the wrong thing. But that's all right. A little bit of healthy confusion never killed a man. If anything, confusion is what keeps the unpredictability factor alive in a relationship. Remember the old war cry, 'Confuse the enemy'? Right.

A well-trained mate is generally the guy who

feels well-loved. Once a man is secure in this area, he is willing to take instructions and co-operate. It's the same principle that operates with semi-intelligent pets. You stroke them often enough, offer them chocolate-chip cookies, acknowledge their presence from time to time and you'll have no problems getting them to do what you want them to—listen attentively. And obey unquestioningly. A well-fed man is more likely to go along with a woman's desires than a guy whose wife starves him or serves him food indifferently. Don't leave the poor chap hungry. Enzymes have a way of creating havoc with one's system. A growling stomach goes with a scowling face. Rule number one in your training programme: regular hot meals served lovingly in a manner that pleases his eyes, nose and palate. Give him what he likes even if you detest cooking it. A man who has been raised on masala karelas will continue to crave for them even if you pull faces and pretend to throw up each time he urges you to taste some. A basic meat-and-potatoes chap remains that forever. Don't believe for a moment that you'll be able to convert him into a Gandhian vegetarian satisfied with dahi-bhaat and lemon pickle on the side. Neither can a glutton become a gourmet. Before you marry a man, get to know his food habits. How much? How many times? How cooked? A lot of marriages fall apart because the partners cannot agree on daily menus. And invariably fight over orders in restaurants. It must also be stated at this point that countless modern marriages have been saved by take-out Chinese.

Food being such a personal and basic requirement, you must never underestimate its importance in your relationship.

To train a man to any level of competence women use (a) food (b) sex (c) food and sex. Food is generally simpler to cater to. If the fellow can't live without his aloos, well, give him the bloody aloos everyday. Use your imagination or Tarla Dalal's recipe book. Learn to dress them up in fifty different ways. But for God's sake let him have them. Depriving a man of his favourite food is to commit a small crime. Dammit, he's paying for the *tarkari*. It's cruel not to let him eat bhajiyas at teatime or ghulab-jamuns on Sunday afternoon because *you* are on a diet. Which is why one cannot emphasize enough the importance of compatible daily diets. I have yet to see a happy non-veg/veg marriage. One or the other of the partners goes through life with a constipated expression—the sufferer's craving for the forbidden food is actually discernible. It's a pretty sorry sight and I've often felt like slipping a doggy bag filled with all the items on the banned list to the deprived soul. Food is what fuels a healthy relationship—even between you and your pets. Seen the blissful look on a puppy's face after he's polished off a bowl full of mince? It's exactly the same expression you'll find in the eyes of a satiated man. In other words, give him a large helping of chana-batura, if that's what turns him on—and *then* issue your first instructions.

It's important to monitor the tone of your voice during the early stages. Don't let your commands sound like commands. Keep them soft and persuasive. Better still, make them appear like his ideas. Look astonished if and when confronted with suspicion. Play dumb. Play injured. Play hurt. 'How could you think I was trying to change you? Don't be ridiculous, I love you the way you are. That's why I married you. I was only trying to say that maybe you shouldn't slurp your rassam/belch as obviously/ tear a chicken apart with both your hands/wipe haldi-stained fingers on a freshly starched napkin/mess up the wash basin after meals/ squash over-ripe bananas into a mound of rice. If you holler at the guy as in 'Gawd! Stop that filthy habit of yours at once. It makes me sick', he isn't going to listen or change. On the contrary, your harshness will put his back up, resulting in his digging his heels in and hollering back, 'If you don't like my eating habits and table manners, go back to your father's house.' Such exchanges serve no purpose. Teach through example. It's the best way. And don't forget the pat on the back/kiss on the cheek/roll in the hay at the end of a constructive session. If you remember to show your appreciation, he will find it worth his while to file away your instructions in his memory bank.

Sex is as effective as food—and women have always married the two. First—the great meal. Then the Big 'F'. Unbeatable. Courtesans never forget that connection. Great seductions are built on partridge and paté, not aloo gobi and sandwiches. Wine helps but only in moderation and preferably of a known vintage. Alcohol is a tricky thing—how much is too much? Off-hand, it would be safe to say that anything more than three glasses of wine is likely to affect the man's sexual performance. A lot of women actively conspire to do just that—promise the object of their seduction a hedonistic night filled with hot sex while plying him with Scotch straight up. The morning after the night before, he'll wake up convinced he's had a great time even if the memory of exactly *what* happened remains hazy.

Sex is an extremely potent weapon which needs to be handled with the utmost care. If you whip it out once too often, it will cease to have the desired effect. If your training programme is to succeed you have to dole it out judiciously or else he'll wise up to what you're doing. He'll *still* want the sex—but he won't change whatever it is that you want him to. Women stuck with borderline alcoholics often use sex as a bait, hoping it will keep their man off the bottle. Does it? Not really. Men who like booze, *like* booze. They aren't about to give it up for a piece of easily available tail—are you kidding? Giving up sex is far easier than giving up booze. Give an alcohol-loving guy the option and if he's truthful he'll tell you he can live without boobs but not his bottle.

To train your mate in this area is one of life's greatest and often most thankless challenges. A lot of women start congratulating themselves prematurely as early as on the honeymoon when their groom insists he'd rather swim in a pair of limpid pools (the babe's eyes) than in a tumbler of Scotch. The pretence is not even worth the sober words he's so earnestly spouting. When the trusting, dewy-eyed bride is enjoying a post-coital shower, the man will in all likelihood be taking a big nip or two out of a carefully hidden quarter-bottle. The signs to watch out for? He's likely to rush past a very wet woman and head straight for the washbasin to gargle out any traces of alcohol. Or he might say he is off for a quick jog (even in a downpour). Other alibis? A work-out in the hotel gym. An unscheduled nap. Or 'some stuff to clear up with the front office manager.' Stuff that can't wait. Okay. Maybe the man really wants to reform and stay off booze. He's decided to be a good boy in all sincerity. A sensitive woman will not mention booze in his presence. Or taunt him about his past 'bad habits'. If she is silly enough to do so— she'll be pushing him to the nearest bootlegger. She will not convert *not* mentioning booze into her mission in life either. And she will not pretend to be an amateur Alcoholics Anonymous volunteer. She will treat booze naturally and lightly. It won't become a forbidden word or topic. She will refrain from cracking jokes about it, but she will not remove every single bottle from their home. The bar will not be declared out of bounds either. If she handles it sensibly he will be more committed to dealing with the situation. If he slips up occasionally she will bite her tongue off but not utter those dreaded words—'I knew it. You've been drinking again.' Two completely obvious and unnecessary statements. She will, instead, smile in a friendly manner, continue to flip through magazines/ watch TV/cook/bathe/talk on the telephone. If she can find it within herself to do so, she'll ask casually. 'Met some friends?' and leave it there. If she adopts that line, the man will feel like an absolute turd and kick himself in the loo. But if she gets aggressive, he'll figure, 'Who needs this nagging? I should never have given the stuff up in the first place.' Getting a guy to go off alcohol requires at least a decade of tender loving care. It cannot be achieved instantly. Not even when romantic love is peaking, like on a honeymoon.

Men resist wifely training with all their might, no matter what the agenda involves. They resist partly because they believe it's the manly thing to do, but mainly because they're afraid other men and their own mother will laugh at them (which of course they do and will). Men will risk ruining their livers rather than get laughed at by their buddies. Besides, men are paranoid about the so-called 'power' of women over their lives. 'No female can change me . . . she has yet to be born,' they boast after their fifth stiff one. In reality they're scared stiff that that's precisely what is happening in their life and that the change has already taken place.

To prove a point—even an absurd one—a man will go to ridiculous lengths. Boozing like there's no tomorrow is one of them. Even after he actually starts detesting the stuff a man will walk towards a bottle, a defiant glint in his eyes . . . and he will glug it all down only because his wife is watching anxiously from the sidelines and his friends are monitoring their respective moves. If he sees disapproval and/or disgust on her face, he will knock back more than he'd intended to in the first place. If she looks indifferent, he'll strive to attract her attention— and knock it back with still more gusto. If she laughs, the reaction will once again be ditto. In simple lingo—when a guy's gotta drink, he's gotta drink. And no force in the world can stop him.

Training your spouse to be a better daddy is far easier. You know why? It's less strenuous for him to pretend to love his kids madly than to feign a lack of interest in alcohol. You can't force fatherly feelings in a man for whom such sentiments do not exist. But societal pressures are such that at some point, the guy will be shamed into being demonstrative and daddy-like, at least when the in-laws are visiting. Encourage every such effort actively. Reward the man (with better and more sex, naturally) and there are good chances that he'll want to repeat the performance.

Men like to *project* themselves as caring, loving providers. It's one of their favourite myths. 'I love my kids . . . my wife . . . my family.' Which man hasn't declared that at least twice during his lifetime? Well, bloody hell, you say to the chap making these declarations, we sure hope you do. What's the big deal? Why the need to shout it from the rooftops? It's not an *achievement* or something, is it?

Wrong. In his eyes it *is* an achievement. It *is* a big deal. Men fancy themselves as essentially solitary creatures braving the unknown alone as they undertake the arduous journey of life. In this fanciful, romanticized and completely fake vision of theirs, there is no place for cumbersome stumbling blocks such as kids. To get them to accept the far-from-fun role of full-time father, is hard indeed. They'd rather hand over a fixed amount of money for the family's upkeep and forget about boring details like responsibilities, duties and obligations. Mothers. What are they there for, they'll ask irritably. It's *their* job to rush a kid with a nose-bleed to the emergency wing of a clinic that happens to be 50 km away. It's also their responsibility to handle school/college admissions, pack lunches, plan holidays, feed, bathe, clean bottoms, counsel, weep, laugh, worry, lose sleep, agonize, beat, scold and generally keep their own lives on hold while the children grow up. The man's part in all this? Heck—he's busting his ass making the money that makes living possible . . . comfortable . . . tolerable. He can't do that and raise the kids as well. That's impossible. And unfair. Oh . . . so the wife works too? So what . . . women make better nurturers. God said so. And so did Mother Dear. Both of them can't possibly be wrong. God, maybe. But not Mummyji. What was that? The wife earns as much? More? Maybe. But that doesn't cancel out her primary concern, which is the family. Sure, her salary pays for all the perks. But that still doesn't exempt her from asking for leave from office when the daughter needs her, or the son wants to be driven to some distant destination. After all, money isn't the answer. A woman must know her priorities. And it was *she* who wanted kids in the first place. Kids. Not kid. Since it was her big idea, well, she just had to deal with it.

Presenting child psychology books to such men is not the way to train them. Lecturing does not produce results either. That induces guilt which is, in any situation, counter-

productive. And negative reinforcement is always
bad news. How many times can a self-respecting
wife holler, 'Look here . . . you too had something
to do with bringing these kids into the world—
remember? Now will you kindly take some time
off from golf and go see your ten-year-old son—
with multiple fractures—before he turns twenty-
one?' Men hate sarcasm. Men hate a lot of
things. But mainly men hate women who point
out their faults.

Does that mean women should hold their
peace forever . . . stay mum . . . and say nothing
at all even under extreme provocation? Precisely.
Say nothing. But don't give up on the training
programme. Be sneaky. Be smart. Be subtle. Do
it right. Create a conscience where none exists . . .
without playing the holy martyr. A long-suffering
mate becomes unbearable after the first fifteen
minutes of the act. Cut that out and get down to
business. Serious business. Make the man believe
that being a good father is somehow sexy. That
you find him irresistible when you see him
changing dirty diapers or burping the baby. Tell
him women go weak in the knees when a man
has a brat as an accessory ('Anybody can wear
a fancy tie or sport cool shades . . . but hey . . .
how many guys look as good with a kid draped
over the shoulder?'). There's nothing like good
old-fashioned vanity to make the man surrender.
Better sense will tell him he's being conned—
but it won't stop the guy from grabbing the baby

and taking off for a long walk without you (taking you along would ruin the impact totally—besides, which young thing is likely to stop and chuck his kid under the chin if *you're* going to be there glowering?). This little trick will buy you enough time to bleach your upper lip, pamper your elbows, chop up the veggies for *dabbas* the next day, iron a few sarees, watch TV in peace or flirt with a neighbour. With any luck it will also create a healthy environment for father and kid to bond. Once the bonding process begins, you can go easy on the training. Something wonderful may stir yet within the beast's heart, and fatherhood—genuine this time—will reign.

Be warned. You may succeed in training your man to do practically anything your heart desires (provided you provide the right incentives) but you'll never be able to get him to love your family just because you love them. If he happens to fall for your sexy kid sister—now that's something else altogether. He may even plump for your sexy old mother. Fine. But it's more likely that your folks will give the guy an allergy. That's how it is.

Do not mope, sulk or make yourself miserable over this. He hates them with good reason—they hate him too. It's mutual. He's the man who has removed you from the family fold. He is the villain who has made you cut your beautiful hair, start drinking, wear awful clothes, restrict your outings and phone calls, sack the old ayah, lose all that lovable puppy fat, stop eating murgh musallam, change your surname.

Basic stuff that irritates family members.

And, as your father will point out even twenty years after you're married, 'Say what you like, *beti*—he is an outsider. A stranger. And will always remain one.' If you have a sense of humour, you'll tell your father off by joking, 'You mean I've been sleeping with a stranger all these years?'

Sometimes, pointing out the obvious does not have the desired effect. You might find your name struck off your father's will. And your mother might refuse to cook your husband's favourite matar-kheema ever again. No. That's far too much of a risk. It's better to start with your husband even if you're doomed to failure.

Rule No. 1: Never sing the praises of your family. You'll be out-of-tune. And he'll be suspicious wondering what you're trying to sell him. Run your family down making it sound like a half-jest. He'll laugh uproariously at their expense and start believing you're on his side after all.

Rule No. 2: Don't call them. They'll call you. Or phone them when he's at work. Sound vague when he asks about their welfare. The moment he discerns over-involvement from your side in 'your people', he'll start resenting even the mention of their names.

Rule No. 3: Do not encourage frequent visits. You know that old chestnut about over-familiarity. Never have pajama parties that include brothers, sisters, nephews or nieces—from your side, that is. If you follow this pattern scrupulously for at least three years, he will relax enough to tolerate their presence without actually breaking out in spots. Once the man is disarmed, the rest is easy—provided your mother doesn't get carried away.

Mothers mean well, but sometimes that's exactly what screws things up. Tell Mummyji to keep the presents coming in at festival time but not to overdo the doting mother-in-law act. In your mother's eyes, he will see the future you. Pray that she goes easy with the war paint and doesn't weep mascara all over his new shirt. After approximately nineteen years of staying away from the two of you, your mother will be tolerated during her annual visits provided she doesn't interfere with your domestics and chase the moody cook out.

The other problem areas so far as training goes concern a man and his friends—he definitely loves a few of them far more than he loves you. Accept that. Do not try and break the bonds which may go back decades. If they are obnoxious drunken louts who pee all over the guest room potty and break wind at the dinner table, too bad. You can't reform them. And your mate won't give them up. If you pull faces at the mention of their names, he will notice immediately—and love them even more. If you say you can't stand them, he'll invite them to spend the very next weekend at your getaway cottage in the hills. And guess who'll have to make twelve-egg omelettes for those beer-drinking boors?

Men feel as sentimental about their buddies as women do about their diamonds. It's absolutely no use pointing out their many faults and shortcomings since men also feign deafness when it comes to criticism about other men who are no better than reflections of their own miserable selves. Clever women stay out of situations that involve (a) heavy drinking (b) weeping nostalgically into martinis (c) watching football games (d) talking shop (e) discussions on cars (f) money matters. These are seen as primarily masculine subjects on which women have no real opinions. If a woman is reckless enough to attempt a tête-à-tête on topics men guard so jealously, she is asking for (1) trouble (2) a snub. Men are childishly possessive about their territories—even if the woman happens to be a brainy broad who knows more about high finance than the lot of them put together. In fact, that makes it worse. Husbands get prickly when it comes to wives who challenge the uninformed views of their friends. 'You made him look small.' 'You were showing off.' 'You humiliated him in front of all of us.' 'What were you trying to prove anyway?' Do you need that? No, you don't. Plus, you don't really want to be inducted into the juvenile club. So, when there is a major 'old boys' get-together, either at your home or someplace else—stay cool. But mainly stay out of it.

If your husband genuinely enjoys the company of assorted low-lives, bums and stiffs—why not be sporting enough to kiss him 'bye-bye' and wish him a pleasant evening? Just as he doesn't have to adore your childhood mates or spend time listening to girlie gossip, you too can learn to switch off and let go. If it's your training schedule you're worried about—hey—concentrate on other, more significant areas. Not trivial stuff like this. Better still—pretend you can't get enough of one of those ughs he enjoys. Laugh uproariously at the man's jokes, hang onto his every word, look deep into his eyes. Do that five times in a row and your mate will gradually ease the man out his charmed circle. Ignore him, be rude about his callow ways, show your disdain, refuse to clear his ashtrays—and you are stuck. Men have strange notions about loyalty. They believe it's heroic to stick together—even if the company they keep stinks. Literally. Well, try distributing free deos for their b.o. Ventilate the room well, before and after. Spray enough cologne to take care of lingering odours. And go spend the evening drinking Margaritas with your favourite companion. Sex of companion: unspecified.

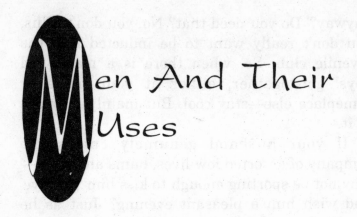

Men And Their Uses

Come on, girls. Be fair. Think hard. Go on. Don't give up. Surely you can come up with at least five things men are good at and can be productively used for? Considering I provided you the clues right at the beginning? Let's start listing them out. (1) Moving heavy furniture around while you issue instructions. (2) Dropping you to your mother's house on a rainy evening. (3) Making love to you when you aren't watching Mel Gibson in *Braveheart* and fantasizing. (4) Paying the bills. (5) Dancing the tango—because it takes two to.

Please add to the list freely and fairly. It's

tough, but if you're in a generous frame of mind, it's actually possible to feel good about a few things about men. Besides, men like to be needed. They like to believe they are useful. There is a scene in the popular soap, *The Bold and the Beautiful*, in which a tough titty of a mother turns to her handsome son and asks forlornly, 'Why do you think your father left me? Wasn't I a good wife? Where did I go wrong?' And the handsome son replies, 'You didn't make him feel needed. You never let him know how much you depended on him. He never saw you cry.' And the old bat promptly bursts into tears. Millions of women the world over, watching this scene, made an instant vow to camouflage their capabilities completely and play helpless in the presence of their mates. An awfully large number of women tested their tear ducts as well, just to ensure they were in working order in case they needed them someday.

It's a pity today's social environment actively discourages a show of naked emotion. Just like tough guys aren't supposed to boogie, tough girls aren't supposed to boo-hoo. Huge mistake. A major tactical error. There's nothing quite as satisfying as a good, long cry. And nothing quite as effective either. Macho men melt like ice cubes under a sunlamp the minute a woman's eyes begin to moisten. Forget the hard-hearted brutes who lack good old-fashioned compassion. They treat us like we treat them—cold-bloodedly.

We are discussing *real* guys with *real* feelings we can tap and use. Women who know when and how much to cry in front of these guys, or more importantly, the point at which to stop—they're the ones who get it all. The goodies and the perks. There is nothing a *well-timed* howling session won't get you, provided you don't look like a crocodile.

A woman-friend once told me how she gets her husband to buy her the most extravagant, unaffordable and obscenely priced gifts. First, she tries the traditional route (a long and hot b.j. on a Sunday afternoon). If that doesn't work, she goes for undisguised flattery ('Ooh! All that tennis is making your calves explode. Just look at them!') If he still prefers to watch Steffi Graf pulping Aranxta Sanchez-Viccario, she bursts into tears and whimpers, 'You don't love me. You don't talk to me. You don't listen. You don't appreciate me . . . have you noticed I've cut my hair? No? I knew it. And you didn't say anything about the new pillow covers either—they're blue. Why blue? Because it's your favourite colour.' By then the guy has completely lost his concentration. Steffi has become a blond blur. He is angry. Furious. He wants to yell. 'Shut the fuck up, woman.' But he doesn't. He walks to the cupboard, takes out his wallet and asks, 'Credit card or cash?' She wipes her tears quickly and beams, 'Well, the saree is for seven thousand. And the pearl bracelet for fifteen . . . you decide.'

The tears have done their trick again.

Don't men see through this cheap trick? Of course, they do. Don't they mind being make bakras of? Some of them. The others? They feel used—and useful.

My friend's husband can't get enough of ass-whipping. He's smart. He understands money. He knows his wife is being a bitch. Does he resent it? No, he tell himself all women are bitches. At least his bitch is beautiful and good in bed. There is a price-tag attached to any service. It's a matter of figuring it out and closing the deal. That's all. That's all?? Yup. For some men, that's all.

There is another equally cunning strategy adopted by a woman I know vaguely. She just spends and and spends and goes on spending without experiencing the slightest remorse or guilt. When an alarmed husband asks for an explanation, she looks astonished. 'I don't believe it. You want to know where all that money has gone? Why? I spent it. I'm your wife . . . I needed all that stuff.' If that doesn't exactly fly, she hugs him and purrs, 'I don't know what it is . . . but I always think of you as a very, very wealthy man. It must be your personality. You look like a super tycoon.' By then, the man has turned to putty, his chest expanded by ten inches, his height increased by three additional feet.

After more sober calculation, he might figure it's better for his wife to return at least a few of her extravagant buys. But he hasn't yet figured that she has already figured out his figuring and bought exactly the double of what she in fact wanted. This way, she gets her loot and he, the poor sucker, feels he has asserted himself.

Women adopt different tactics to achieve different targets. They don't see this as 'using' men. It's their rightful due that they're recovering by slightly unorthodox means, that all. They argue that if men were less mean and just handed them whatever they were clamouring for, they wouldn't have to resort to such tricks in the first place. True. Which may be why another lady just goes ahead and buys herself fabulous gifts for her birthday and their anniversary. She is considerate enough to pass on all the bills to her husband or at least inform him that she has more or less cleaned out their joint account. With that task out of the way, she feels lighter and better. 'How can anybody call this "using"?' some women demand indignantly. 'Don't men use us when we fetch, carry, cook and clean for them? Do they compensate us for all our work?' No, they don't. They won't. And they never will. Why? Because men genuinely believe that God created women specially to keep the toilets sparkling and offer their bodies for penetration as and when. A lot of women accept and embrace these premises too, because they also believe they've been placed on this earth to do just that—clean and fuck. 'Why has

God given us legs?' they ask rhetorically. 'Obviously, to walk from the kitchen to the bedroom.' It's the ones who disagree that land themselves either in a mess or alone. Generally alone.

Use No. 1: Moving furniture has become so much easier now with the new lightweight Plexigas models—even kids can push those around like lego blocks. In the old mahogany days, moving home or even rearranging stuff used to require stealth, planning, cunning and . . . sex. It's still sex. To get a man to shift a chair from place A to place B, it's not enough to promise him a tava dosa and filter coffee later. He can get that anyway, anytime. Besides, these days, there's a good chance of him saying. 'Move the bloody chair yourself. Or just leave it where it is.' You can remind him about the number of times he has stubbed his toe while lurching towards the refrigerator in the dark, all because of that same 'bloody chair'. Will that make him heave and shove at your behest? Naah. Next time he does stub his toe, he'll cuss away as he always does, yell in pain and remember his grandmother. But he will *not move the chair*.

Unless you use certain inducements. Like sex. When all else fails, try sex. He may still refuse to move the chair . . . but the success ratio improves greatly after a b.j. for a job that will eventually be done.

Men hate to push cars and display not the

slightest shame while you get out (often in pouring rain) to get the damn vehicle moving. 'I need to be at the steering wheel,' the chap will say without blinking. Don't argue. Keep pushing. It's an ego thing. It's not manly to be seen behind a car heaving away while a pregnant wife stands forlornly at the kerb and a scruffy mechanic handles the wheel. The logic defeats me, but it is somehow more manly for the guy to be at the wheel while the same pregnant wife (with or without a mechanic) uses her bloated strength to get the car engine to splutter to life. It's not at all impossible for a man to get so excited when the car starts that he zooms off into the distance completely forgetting about the preggie woman who has made it possible in the first place . . . and leave her standing on the wet road clutching her belly.

They don't intend to be sadistic or mean. It's just that men tend to be a little forgetful about details. But if you know how to press the right buttons (the man's not the car's) you'll never have a problem with either furniture or beat-up jalopies. Playing helpless used to work a couple of centuries ago but there were no cars, only horse carriages then. Today, helpless babes get nowhere except on everybody's nerves. A woman has two options (a woman always has two options). She can work out at a good gym and build up her biceps so she can move her own bloody chair, or she can stick to minimalist decor and taxis.

Dhurries, gaddies or tatami mats are perfect for women who have no real use for men anyway. As for sex, there *are* some women who state vehemently that they are perfectly capable of pleasuring themselves, thank you. They do it on their own time, at their own pace, using methods that reach all the right spots and climaxing when they're good and ready to. Besides, mechanical devices rarely snore, smoke or ask stupid questions like 'How was it for you?'

Use No. 2: Men as escorts. Heck—that's pretty outdated already. Liz Taylor needs a walker. Madonna requires minders. Sridevi is reported to have cornered another woman's husband. What earthly use do chicks have for regular male escorts in these times? We aren't talking husbands and boyfriends here. Just escorts. Even the swishiest of joints welcome single females/female couples/female groups. They drink and smoke much more. Eat enormous amounts. Laugh tantalizingly. Make eyes at dishy waiters. Flirt with the maitre d'. Leave huge tips (it's easy after six tequilas). Dance sexily with one another (remember Sharon Stone and partner in *Basic Instinct?*) and add considerably to the glamour quotient of the place. So . . . who needs escorts?

On holidays? Ummm. Yes and no. Men can really screw up and screw up bad—on vacations. They think they know a lot about airline schedules, discounts, room rates, deals, bargains and such stuff that lousy holidays are made of. Actually, they know zuck. Women are far more organized when it comes to travel arrangements—except that the men in their lives have a mental block about seeing it that way.

So, a woman sportingly accepts her spouse's suggestion to share a mini-van with another family staying at the hotel only to discover that the youngest kid in that family is suffering from something highly contagious or disgustingly messy. It's always a toss-up between whooping cough and diarrhoea. Does a good wife protest? Flag down a passing pickup truck? Get off and hitch a ride back to the resort? Contact her lawyer? Make eyes at the only camel-owner in the desert who can save her from the kid?

Nothing of the sort.

She grits her teeth, smiles sweetly and says to herself, 'At least I have a husband. An escort. A companion. Yes, he's goofed up our holiday. My bladder is bursting. The vein in my forehead is throbbing dangerously. I'm about to puke all over my new jeans. And someone will need to restrain me physically before I tear that kid to pieces. Other than that—I'm so lucky I've got my man with me.'

Sure. More often than not men make lousy travelling-companions. Their bladders function differently. And they're constantly looking for a drink. They get airline schedules mixed up, and often leave passports and other important documents at home. They get dazed, disoriented and downright stupid while dealing with immigration/customs pigs at international airports. They generally pass on their tension to the family which ends up disgracing itself, its forefathers and its country on foreign soil. All because the man of the house can't handle simple procedures like filling in disembarkation cards.

What does a super-efficient wife do in these circumstances? She plays deaf and dumb. She pretends she hasn't heard the snigger from the swine behind the counter. She smiles engagingly at the son-of-a-bitch who forces her to open all the suitcases (the keys, naturally, can't be found because daddy had taken charge of them before departure). She even tries her schoolgirl German/French/Italian on the surly cab-driver who she knows is going to rook them anyway. All this she does without letting the man feel threatened/foolish/small. It's 'their' holiday and it must not begin on the wrong note or else she will be blamed for every tiny thing. Little does she know that she's going to be blamed for everything regardless. But since separate holidays (like separate bedrooms) are still not popular, women have no choice but to put up with men who'll give them grief even on their precious days off.

That is the downside. The good stuff lies in

having someone to get the baggage on and off conveyor belts, flag down a taxi while hanging on to a frisky trolley . . . and find a long, cool drink when you most need it. It's also safer to walk into a bar (swishy or otherwise) with a man who is obviously a husband leading the way. Unless you are looking to be picked up in which case you don't need anything more than a pair of fuck-me shoes and red lipstick.

Random Uses: All right. To sum up. Men are good at starting fires. Training dogs. Clipping obstinate toenails. Taking lipstick off your teeth. Standing guard outside strange loos without latches. Selecting bras. Sampling new dishes. Approving your choice in curtains. Untangling hair. Getting grit out of your eyes. Fixing cocktails. Filing tax returns. Filing nails. Filing divorce papers. Taking the dog to the vet's. Recycling lousy gifts. Opening champagne bottles. Valet parking. Tipping waiters and barbers. Firing servants. Hiring servants. Massaging the small of your back. Powdering unreachable areas. Summoning the TV repairman in the middle of the night. Kicking ass. Soldiering on when you're ready to give up. Helping you quit smoking. Picking shirts for your father. Paying hospital bills. Replacing fuses. Stopping leakages. Reserving comments on your lousy haircut. Helping you make up with a bitchy sister. Swatting monsoon flies. Replacing mosquito-repellent mats. Hanging pictures. Taking down pictures. Re-hanging the same pictures. Making love in the shower. Discouraging you from driving. Kissing you with night cream slathered all over your face.

Really, men *do* have their uses. Only you have to identify them correctly. And know when and where to stop. But that's like expecting a man to do likewise with his whiskies. An unrealistic hope. But hey—you did say you liked four-letter words, didn't you?

Things Our Mamas Didn't Have To Do For Men

Mainly, yes mainly, our mamas didn't have to work hard at being 'good in bed'. Oh no. It was enough that our mamas were in bed at all and not in the kitchen slaving over a dekchi full of khichdi—when what the man was looking for was a different dish altogether. Our mamas were let off quite lightly. If their men didn't like what they were getting, they had two clear choices—to lump it, or opt for lifelong celibacy. Straight, simple options.

They also had a third, but few dared to

exercise it: paid sex. For one thing, prostitution fell into the disorganized sector. For another it required far too much of an effort. The men could maintain a mistress if they had the means. They could go off to various *mandis* and visit nautch girls over weekends. Or they could sleep with servant girls/poor relatives/sisters-in-law/goats and other pets. But mainly, they slept with their wives—such as they were. It was clearly sex on a woman's terms way back then.

For example:

• Our mamas didn't necessarily have to keep the lights on when they 'did it'.

• They almost invariably kept their sarees on while 'doing it'.

• They didn't have to wax/shave/thread anything. Hair was considered natural.

• They rarely wore undies. So the question of owning the entire range of 'Victoria's Secret' in plum, purple, burgundy and acid green was avoided.

• They didn't have Sharon Stone/Madonna/Sridevi as model bed-mates they were expected to mimic. Which meant no grunts, no screams, no scratches, no bites . . . and best of all, no daggers/knives/ice-picks concealed under the marital bed.

• They didn't have to fake it if they didn't make it. Men had few expectations. It was enough just to have a woman in the bed—and never mind if she wasn't Pamela Anderson.

- Women didn't have to compete with television during sex. There *was* no television to distract their men.

- They didn't have to be anorexic for their guys to get turned on. *Au contraire*, buxom, well-fed women with rounded buttocks and thick waists were considered the real sex bombs.

- This meant that women were freed from subjecting their bodies to punishing diets/bouts of bulimia/near starvation. Since their appetite for food was not suppressed, neither was their appetite for the other, less-yummy stuff.

- Women had to follow a fairly easy route to make a success of their marriage—regular *khana-peena-dena*, hot meals, cold beverages and sex-on-demand. Not too much to ask for in return for a roof over one's head, twelve sarees and some jewellery.

- Sex wasn't discussed ad nauseum. It didn't matter whether men were from Mars and women from Venus . . . so long as the bills were paid at the end of the day. And the kids weren't on the streets. Sex was something people did, not talked about.

- They didn't have to bathe with their men, climb into a jacuzzi, shower with fragrant gels, and get all sexy during a body massage. They were far too busy keeping the kids out— especially since bedrooms doors were rarely locked.

- They didn't have to bleach their upper lips

or floss regularly.

• They saved on lingerie, make-up, rich night creams, perfumes, body lotions, deos, satin sheets, Calvin Klein—everything. All they had to do was hitch up their sarees, shut their eyes and think of Dilip Kumar.

So much for sex.

Look at all the other stuff they could give two fingers to. Our mamas didn't have to host or attend cocktail parties for reasons of 'bijness'— their husbands' 'bijness'. They didn't have to go for high-profile 'events' either (the biggest 'event' for them being their own wedding, with the next twenty-five years spent on planning the other 'event'—their son's wedding). Socially, they had a mariginal role to play. They were just 'wives' and were expected to look and act like, well . . . wives. Conversation was restricted to uttering 'Haanji' or 'Really ji?' at the right moments, laughing discreetly at the husband's jokes, restraining the children from picking their noses in front of guests and making sure there were hot pakoras with the drinks.

They didn't have to compete in the cuisine stakes either. Who ever ate tacos? Who served Thai? Who'd even heard of sashimi? Did it matter whether the food was home-cooked or catered? Did mama have to mix perfect Margaritas? Did she have to dance the Macarena? Was she expected to be on high-powered committees? Get her name in some crappy society columns? Know exactly where to shop in Acapulco? Make sure her hair roots were always well camouflaged with the latest auburn rinse? Be on first-name terms with European chefs at posh local restaurants? Speak to Japanese collaborators in their own lingo?

Hell, no. Her husband was happy enough if she smiled pleasantly at visitors. Remembered not to belch in their faces. Stuffed the boss with deep-fried snacks (that would send the author of *Fit for Life* into orbit). And presented the guest with a Banarasi silk scarf with gold motifs (from 'Cottage Industries only') for his 'missus'.

No such luck for today's hostesses, I'm afraid. If they cannot whip up a gourmet meal themselves, they must at least know who to call up. Wine? Excuse me—but you have to brush up on your Bordeaux vintages before that hellish sit-down at 'The Zodiac Grill'. What would the suave Savio think otherwise? No Kishco either. It's Christofle or nothing. Details. Everything is in that dreaded 'D' word. Get them (details) right and go straight to the kingdom in the sky that welcomes 'good' wives. For that privilege you have to earn your Brownie points right here on earth. Do you really think trophy wives are born in the shape of gleaming silver cups or impressive shields? They get that way through hard work that involves a lot of kneeling. Back-breaking work, really. The sort of work mom never dreamt of. But that's because mom never got to see soft-porn. She didn't know the existence of phone-sex either. Nor did she have girlfriends close enough to discuss sex-secrets with. Poor mom. She had to fall back on her instincts— which may or may not have been basic. But even she must have had her moments—like when the hubby actually noticed she had breasts, for example. And they weren't meant exclusively for suckling infants.

Mom provided wholesome daal-chaval. She cooked. She cleaned. She made babies: And she kept her man happy. *That was her goddamned role in life*, for Chrissake. So where exactly did *we* fuck up? Who changed the lines? Who rescripted the screenplay? Who messed up? Thousands and thousands of women are looking back nostalgically and weeping. This isn't what they wanted at all. This wasn't what they were *told* would happen if they became 'today's women'. This wasn't part of the deal. They've been conned. And conned big. They want their money back. Money? What money? Their own frigging money, all right? The stuff they've made themselves. What about it? Well—it's theirs. And they want it. Too bad. It's gone. No receipts. Nothing.

That's another thing mom didn't have to lose hair over—money. Daddy made it, she spent it. Simple. Well, she didn't blow it up on herself. She spent it on the family. Things are different now. Mom makes money too—and what is she expected to do with her lolly? 'What my husband makes is mine. And what I make is mine as well,' says a bright career person and means it. Is that how it really works? Surprise, surprise— yes. But she's an exception. Mom scrupulously maintained accounts. And she didn't need a computer to tell her how to balance her books. She had her little diary in which she noted all the expenses. Daddy occasionally glanced at it (just to keep mom on her toes) and the marriage worked.

No more. Today, it's strictly his and her accounts. Cheque-books are guarded more strictly than old love letters. Wives refuse to let their husbands get even a teeny-weeny look-see at their balance sheets.

Mom doesn't understand this—she wants to know why her daughter needs to go out and earn a living in the first place. Isn't that what marriage and men are for? So, the daughter goes into the self-worth, self-image explanation. It doesn't convince mom. 'Men are supposed to pay for, everything, *beti*,' she says in puzzlement. 'Not today's men,' the daughter reminds her. Mom shakes her head. 'I don't understand—if the man isn't paying for anything—not even your *khana-peena*—then where does *dena* come into the picture?' Oops. Mom has done it again. Asked an awkward question to which there is no answer. The daughter feels miserable. It is something she has been asking herself, too. She withdraws sexual favours. The husband sulks. 'You are getting it for free,' the woman screams, 'it's not fair!' 'You mean you want me to pay you for it?' the husband demands. 'There's no such thing as a free fuck,' she sneers. 'Oh baby. Excuse me. But I expect a far bigger bang for my money than what I get from you. Therefore, goodbye!' the husband roars. End of story. End of marriage. Mom should never have opened that big mouth of hers.

Speaking of mouths, bet mom never had to perform you-know-what on dad either. Mom didn't have to perform, period. She was lucky. And well-fed (oh well, fat). No aerobics. No health clubs. No sweat. She was just mom. The kids loved her even on her bad hair days. Dad loved her even when she burnt the baingans. And more importantly, she loved herself. So what do we do with our lousy lives now that we can't go back to being our moms, huh??

Epilogue

I received an interesting phone call recently. It was from an ex-colleague. He happened to be in an uncharacteristically chatty mood. Understandably so. The man was getting married. I put it down to nervous chatter. It was a second marriage for him, and his bride-to-be was an ambitious, driven, power-lady, from what he told me. Just like his first wife. So . . . how was it going to be any different this time round? Sounded depressingly like a repeat performance to me. 'No,' said the man emphatically. Tell me about it, I thought cynically.

The date was set for the following week. We were invited. I couldn't wait. Especially since I had my ex-colleague's earlier words ringing in my ears. After a bitterly contested divorce, he had vowed to devote the rest of his life to rugby. I thought he'd made a very sensible choice. Much easier getting in and out of scrums with a group of over-energetic men than dealing with demanding wives or girlfriends in and out of bed. My respect for the man had gone up. Post-divorce, he looked fit, happy, relaxed and sexually fulfilled. Now he was telling me he was ready to give it all up for another shot at what had obviously been a lousy experience—marriage.

Fortunately, the euphoric couple had opted for a low-key wedding and not a social circus. As we walked into the venue, I tried to picture the bride. She probably resembled his first wife. Men tend to go for 'types' rather than individuals. That's why they make the same mistake several times over. One look at the svelte, smartly dressed, very glamorous bride told me I was dead right. He had done it again—married a younger, prettier, shrewder version of the original. This woman was destined to give my friend grief. I could see it in her darting eyes as she networked her way through the crowded room—he was entirely incidental. It was her turn in the spotlight. As for him, he resembled a foolish, deliriously happy doggy-woggy who'd been fed a bowl of baby food and had his muzzle gently wiped. I thought I spotted a tail wagging away as he went around eagerly accepting congratulations from skeptical well-wishers like me.

I decided the marriage was doomed even before it had taken off. She was likely to chew him up within the first few months and spit out the bones. Poor guy, I concluded. A real sucker for good looks and sharp brains: the most lethal combination.

He came up to me with a goofy smile. I waited for the dreaded question. It was coming. It had to come. It did. 'What do you think of her?' This is one of the worst questions to ask a friend. Especially if you don't want a truthful answer—and nobody really does. A newly-married person wants only reaffirmation and reassurance. A pat on the back. A prize. A certificate. A medal. That sort of thing. Insincerely, I tried to do just that—validate his choice, desperately searching for the right-sounding words: not too gushy, but not obviously cynical either. Neutral phrases and bland compliments. The man stopped me mid-sentence. 'Look,' he said, 'I know exactly what you're thinking even without you saying it. "This is not going to work. She's all wrong for him. Why is he doing it? Horrible mistake. They're both going to regret it." Right?' I nodded sheepishly. (Hey— we were friends. Why bullshit the guy?) And that's when he surprised me. 'Listen,' he said, pushing me into a corner for a bit of privacy. 'We're Indian, okay? And we've both known what it's like to cow down to many of our traditions. Well, I've found a. way of turning some of those traditions on their head to suit me. Remember the one that enjoins women to walk six paces behind their man? And the later wisdom that explains that such women are the ones who call the shots in the marriage?'

I was for a long moment mystified. What was he talking about? All right, I knew about the business of walking so many paces behind your man: it's an ancient Indian trick. Our villagers are so good at it, they've managed to convince the rest of us citywallahs too. The village women have been able to fool their poor husbands—those asses toiling in the fields all day round the year under a hot sun. What happens to these men when they go back to their homes? Their meek-looking wives turn into tigresses in the privacy of their huts . . . and the men, too tired to challenge them, submit passively to all their demands—sexual and financial. The next morning the wife covers her face modestly as she heads for the village well and makes sure she stays in her husband's shadow, head downcast, eyes lowered—she has no complaints. Her sexual appetite is sated. Her belly is full. And so is her purse.

But how do you extend the scenario? Superimpose it on the urban marriage? See it in today's context? Especially in a man's?

And then came the clincher. My friend looked at me naughtily, his eyes twinkling, and said,

'Watch me. *I've decided to walk six paces behind my wife for the rest of my life.*'

That was smart thinking. I don't know whether he'll be able to stick to his plan of action for long, but at least he'd seen through the old ruse and turned it around to his advantage. All I could do was wish him luck.

On the way home from the wedding reception, I thought about his strategy. And felt seriously worried. If more men were to start thinking along these lines, we women would be in serious trouble. For centuries we have managed to survive using every known trick in the (unwritten) book—including the one about walking six paces behind the man—what if an entire generation of men tried to subvert our age-old stratagem with its high success-rate? What if our well-laid plans were to be used against us? What if 'they' (the enemies we willingly sleep with) were to beat us at our own game?

They'll do so at their own peril.

But let's not spoil the ending for them.